COOKING &
EATING WITH
BEER

PETER LA FRANCE

COOKING & EATING WITH BEER

50 Chefs, Brewmasters, and Restaurateurs Talk about Beer and Food

JOHN WILEY & SONS, INC.

NEW YORK   CHICHESTER   WEINHEIM   BRISBANE   SINGAPORE   TORONTO

Copyright © 1997 by Peter LaFrance

Published by John Wiley & Sons, Inc.

Library of Congress Cataloging-in-Publication Data
LaFrance, Peter.
     Cooking and eating with beer: 50 chefs, brewmasters and
  restaurateurs talk about beer and food / Peter LaFrance.
        p.   cm.
     Includes indexes.
     ISBN **0-471-31879-5** (cloth: alk. paper)
     1. Cookery (Beer)   2. Beer.   I. Title: Cooking and eating with beer.
  TX726.3.L33   1997
  641.6'23--DC21   96-49039

Printed in the United States of America

10 9 8 7 6 5 4 3 2

To my wife, Virginia, and daughter, Mary

Contents

Preface

The idea for this book developed while I was doing research for a book called *Beer Basics*. While gathering information for the chapter on how to best serve beer and food together, I learned that Chef John Doherty, of the Waldorf Astoria, had presented four "Beer Dinners" before I interviewed him late in 1994 and was planning to do many more. At the Water Club, another fine-dining restaurant in New York City, Chef Rick Moonen was using beers in the recipes on his dinner menu, and beverage manager Sam Corenti had developed a beer list to complement Chef Moonen's menu. To help in my research, these three gentlemen suggested a number of other chefs and restaurateurs who, they assured me, were also looking at beer in a new light. Everyone I spoke to was fascinated by the many different styles of beers available, especially the rich, full-bodied beers from "microbrewers". These unique, flavorful, beers married well with many diverse dishes: subtly flavored or spicy, basic or complex.

Also, at that time, the number of microbreweries, brewpubs and brewery-restaurants operating in the United States and Canada had grown to five hundred and growing. Two tenths of the domestic beer market (one of the largest beer markets in the world) was being brewed by these breweries. The regional and middle-level breweries (in size and volume of beer produced) were also growing in numbers. What convinced many observers that this was not a "flash in the pan" fad was when the top three major breweries (Anheuser-Busch, Coors, and Miller) expanded their own product lines to include a line of what they called "craft-brewed" beers.

Soon fine-dining restaurants began offering beer, as well as wine, to serious diners. Restaurants across the United States and Canada began holding "beer dinners". Here was an opportunity for a local brewer and chef to both show their talents in the best light. What is happening is the celebration of good food, and dining well, and an appreciation of how well the variety of beers available can enhance good food; when mixed in equal measure with good friends and good conversation.

This book presents over fifty chefs, brewmasters and restaurateurs discussing the basics of enjoying beer and good food. When a particular dish is mentioned, and printed in bold typeface, the recipe for that dish can be found in the recipe section of this book. These conversations will begin focused on the general experience of cooking with beer and developing menus that match beers with foods that causes that synergy that realistically approximates perfection. Then the menu will be explored in detail. Each section of the menu focuses on a specific food.

Acknowledgments

I would like to thank the following people who made this book possible: Claire Thompson, for her faith in me; and my wife Virginia, and daughter Mary for understanding and dealing with all the fits and sparks that keep those who live with an author on their toes.

Every chef, restaurateur and brewer who helped with this book has my thanks. Special thanks to Katherine Mary Twyford for her help in translating recipes, Cory Hill for his help making sense of recipes that needed to be adapted to the home kitchen.

Thanks also to the management and staff of "Broome Street Bar", and every other server who has ever placed a glass of beer in front of me. Without these fine people I would have had to do my research in a library.

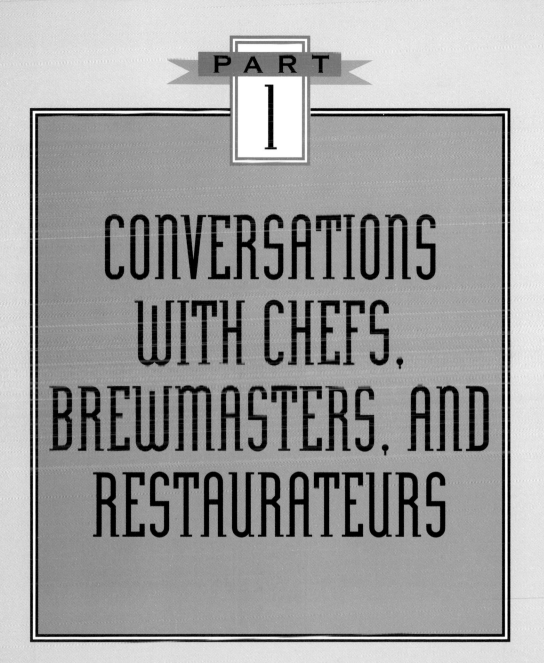

PART

1

CONVERSATIONS WITH CHEFS, BREWMASTERS, AND RESTAURATEURS

Introduction

Good food and good beer form, in every sense of the word, a perfect "marriage." This is not an idle metaphor. In the beginning brewing was the domain of the woman of the house. A household was measured by the quality of food and drink provided by a host. Well-brewed beer was almost always the sign of a healthy family. In those days the local water supply was, more often than not, polluted. Since brewing involves boiling the combination of water, malt sugars, and, later, hop flowers for flavor, it follows then that those with well-brewed beer were healthier than those who drank water. (I have included a brief history of beer in the next section of this book for those who are interested in learning more.)

The natural pairing of the best brew with the best food at the table has led to some classic combinations: weisswurst and Hefe-Weizen Austrian ale, caviar and Czech Pilsner, Belgian Abbey ale and carbonade flammande (almost the Belgian national dish), pizza and Moretti La Rosa, and a good number of the recipes you will find in this book. From humble beginnings, the marriage of beer and food has once again caught the popular imagination.

My aim in writing this book is to offer an intensive look at what is involved in the "perfect" pairing of beer and food. A general introduction to what beer is, and how it is brewed, is followed by a review of the beer and food scene. Knowing what you are working with, and how it is made, is often just as important as the techniques used in the preparation of food.

In traditional kitchens it has long been known that chefs must be careful not to use certain ingredients in certain dishes, because the flavors of those ingredients clash with the wine served with the meal, literally changing its flavor. For example, serving a fine red wine with a salad dressed in a vinaigrette changes the flavors of both the wine and the salad. The result is that the fine wine has no chance to show its best attributes, and the salad seems to take on rather unpleasant flavors. When serving beer, there is much more latitude with the variety of spices, dressings, and sauces that can be used.

Wine is basically categorized as either white or red. The variations are sparkling, still, and the sweet or dessert wines.

Beer, on the other hand, is much more dramatic in its various styles, ranging from the palest pilsners to the deep garnet color of stout. The dramatic range of flavors is matched by an equally dramatic range of alcohol content (from 3.2% to over

12% by weight). Finally, beer is perceived as being a much more "accessible" beverage than wine. There are no growths to memorize, no vintage charts to keep track of, and the price of even the most expensive bottle of beer is considerably less than a wine of similar stature.

This book is organized to resemble a menu because beer goes with everything on the menu. The chefs who spoke with me while I was researching this book were all emphatic on that point. Even those who work in the most sophisticated kitchens enjoy beer with the food they serve.

Each chapter begins with a brief overview of the basic dishes that will be discussed, and the basic techniques for preparing these dishes. Of course, there are differences of opinion on just how far to take the use of beer in many of these dishes. There is also much discussion on how far to take the use of beer in the kitchen in general. Finally, there is a great deal of discussion on which particular beer goes with each dish. I have gone to considerable length to let the chefs themselves carry this debate.

I can assure you that although I have finished writing this book I am still listening, still tasting, and still researching all the variations and pairings included herein. I hope you too will be caught up in the excitement and the discovery.

CHAPTER 1

Beer Basics

Before we begin broiling, braising, stewing, sautéing, and baking, it might be a good idea to take a close look at our basic products.

Beer is basically a fermented drink made from grain, hops, water, and yeast. All beer is made with these four basic ingredients. The next step is to understand that there are over 100 distinct styles of beer brewed in world. To keep things simple, we will be concentrating on the sixteen basic styles of beer most often encountered on the market today.

First we'll look at the basic ingredients, and the process of brewing beer. Then we will explore the different styles of beers and their distinctive personalities. Finally, we will have a chance to discover how much fun it is to match the unique personalities of your favorite beers with your favorite foods.

This book has been written primarily for the North American reader, especially those in the United States. The beers that are featured in this book, unless otherwise noted, are sold in retail shops in most regions of the United States. If you cannot find a particular beer mentioned, you should check with your retailer, or their wholesaler, and ask for it. You might be pleasantly surprised.

Of special interest to both novice and experienced cooks and beer aficionados: this book is indexed, and cross-indexed, so that you have ready access to information on specific beers, recipes, restaurants, and chefs. This should make it easy to find specific information, as well as develop a complete overview of particular styles of beer and cooking.

WHAT IS BEER?

Quite simply, beer is fermented, hop-flavored, malt sugar. There are four basic building blocks needed to make beer: water, malted barley, hops, and yeast.

Yeast (often listed as a fourth ingredient, although not a part of the finished product) is used to ferment the hop-flavored malt sugar tea into an effervescent liquid with an average of 3–7% ethyl alcohol by weight. (In some cases, such as a barley wine, the alcohol content can go as high as almost 11% by weight.) Both beer and ale are made from essentially the same four building blocks, with the major variation being the type of yeast used to ferment the product.

The following is a brief description of the four important building blocks of beer.

WATER

Water comprises over 90% of beer. In the past, the mineral content of natural springs, or artesian wells, constituted a major flavor factor in the beers that were produced in a specific region. Examples of naturally occurring water supplies that have resulted in distinctive beer styles are found at: Burton-on-Trent in the United Kingdom (where Bass Ale is brewed) and Esopus in New York State (a 19th–century brewing center).

Today, brewmasters can chemically adjust any water to create the exact "style" of beer desired. The chemicals added to the water are most often mineral salts such as gypsum or Epsom salts. These salts cause the hop oils to develop specific pronounced flavor characteristics that enhance their use as flavoring agents.

Although the phrase "pure water" has been used extensively in advertisements for beers and ales, every brewery carefully adjusts the water they use to meet their specific flavor profile.

MALTED BARLEY

Barley, a basic cereal grain, is low in gluten, and is not particularly good for milling into flour that is used in bakery products that need gluten, in concert with yeast, to work. There are three major types of barley. Each is differentiated by the number of seeds that grow at the top of the stalk. Barley seeds grow in two, four, and six rows, along a central stem.

European brewers prefer two-row barley because it malts best and has a better starch/husk ratio. Brewers in the United States prefer the six-row barley because it is more economical to grow and has more of the enzymes needed to convert the starch in the grain into sugar and other fermentables. The barley grains must be "malted" before they can be used in the brewing process.

Malting is a process of bringing grain to the point of its highest possible starch content by allowing it to begin to sprout roots and take the first step to becoming a photosynthesizing plant. At this point the seed is rich in the starch it needs to use as food for growth.

When the maximum starch content is reached, the maltster stops the growth process by heating the grain to a temperature that stops growth but allows the important natural enzyme diastase (which converts starch into sugar) to remain active. Barley, once malted, is very high in the type of starches that diastase (found naturally on the surface of the grain, just under the husk) can convert quite easily into a rich sugar called maltose. This sugar is metabolized by the ale or lager yeast to create carbon dioxide (CO_2) and ethyl alcohol.

Portions of this malted barley are then heated at higher temperatures to "roast" it. This roasted malted barley no longer has the active enzymes needed to turn the starches into sugars, but it does take on characteristics that add to the flavor of the beer.

The degree of roasting results in malted barley that ranges from light tan (Dortmund and Bavarian) to patent and chocolate malt (roasted until almost black). These roasted malts add flavor and color to both ales and lager-style beer.

YEAST

Yeast is the organism that metabolizes the sugar (maltose) in the wort into ethyl alcohol and carbon dioxide (CO_2). The fermentation process occurs in two steps. The "primary" fermentation converts most of the maltose to ethyl alcohol and CO_2.

The "secondary" fermentation finishes metabolizing the remaining sugar into the CO_2 necessary to give the beer effervescence.

In traditional beer making, there is also a "priming" that restarts the last of the fermentation in the bottles or kegs. This priming assures that the beer has natural carbonation. In mass-produced commercial beers and ales, the carbonation is injected into the beer when it is bottled or kegged.

There are two kinds of yeast used in fermenting brew:

Ale Yeast: (*Saccharomyces cerevisiae*) An aerobic yeast that needs contact with oxygen to ferment, so it forms a thick layer at the top of the wort. It also works best when the ambient temperature is 60-65°F. Its fermentation also produces esters. These are flavors that can create the essence of apples, pears, and sometimes plums.

Lager Yeast: (*Saccharomyces uvarum*) An anaerobic yeast that ferments at the bottom of the wort and functions best at temperatures of 35-40°F. It produces few esters and takes much longer than ale yeast to complete fermentation.

ADJUNCTS

Although malt and hops are the main contributors to the flavor of beer and ale, in some cases there are additional flavors. Depending on whether you are drinking a beer or an ale, you will also detect flavors that are created by the yeast during fermentation. The ale yeast creates esters that smell like apples, bananas, pears, and oranges.

Lager yeast creates much fewer esters, predominately grassy or new-mown hay or, in some cases citric aromas. These esters are the exception rather than the rule because lager yeast ferments the sugars much more thoroughly than ale yeasts. Lager yeast takes at least 32 days to complete fermentation, while ale yeast takes a week at most.

HOW BEER IS MADE

Beer (both lager and ale) is made in a brew house, which consists of a grist mill, mash tun, copper, fermenter, fermenting tanks, conditioning tanks, and usually a kegging or bottling line. In the case of a brewpub there is no bottling or kegging so the beer is drawn to the tap directly from the conditioning tanks.

The traditional brewery (building containing a brew house) was built on at least three levels. This was done to allow gravity to do much of the work of moving the grain, grist, mash, wort, and spent grains. It was also important that the fermenting and conditioning tanks be in cellars where the temperature was optimum for fermenting and conditioning the beer.

Ale can be fermented and conditioned at higher temperatures than lager, but both need cool, stable temperatures to produce the best product.

GRIST

The first step is to crush the grain into grist. The grain is rolled between metal rollers that are set a specific distance apart so that the crushing is done without turning the grain into flour. The grain should be crushed just enough to allow for optimum extraction of the fermentable sugars from the grain when hot water "liquor" is added to create the mash. The crushing also leaves the husk of the grain intact so that it can form a bed at the bottom of the large kettle where the mash is allowed to convert the starch in the grain into sugars and fermentable substances. This large metal container (often copper-clad to efficiently distribute heat to the mash) is called the mash tun.

When the mash is done, as much of the starch as possible has been converted to sugars and fermentable substances. The liquid in the mash tun is drained through the bed of husks and spent grain remains in the bottom of the mash tun. This sweet liquid is now called wort.

Now hot water/liquor is sprayed on the grains that are left in the mash tun after the wort has been drained. This process, called *sparging*, is done to extract as much fermentables as possible.

THE MASH

The crushed grain (grist) is shoveled into the mash tun where hot liquor (water), heated to approximately 175°F, is added. This is the striking temperature and is a few degrees higher than the optimum mash temperature of about 150-152°F. However, this is the best temperature for the enzymes found naturally in the grain to turn the starches, which make up most of the grain, into maltose (malt sugar) that is fermented by the yeast later in the process.

The temperature range of the mash creates the optimum environment for the enzyme diastase to convert the starch in the malted barley into sugar and other nonfermentable products. Lower temperatures usually produce more nonfermentables; higher temperatures mean less nonfermentable products. These nonfermentables give the finished beer "body," or "mouth-feel."

THE BOIL/BREW

At this point the sweet liquor, now called wort, is piped into a kettle where it is boiled, with the hops, until the proteins are extracted from the wort and the essential oils are extracted from the hops. The hopped wort is then quickly chilled to around 60°F and piped into fermenting tanks.

FERMENTATION

The fermenting tanks (traditionally open in a clean room) are filled with the cool wort and then either top-fermenting or bottom-fermenting yeast is "pitched" (added) and fermentation takes place.

Basically, this is when the yeast metabolizes the sugar in the wort and the resulting products are ethyl alcohol and carbon dioxide.

CARBONATION/FINISHING

When almost all the fermentable sugar has been changed into ethyl alcohol and CO_2 the brew is piped into special "finishing tanks," where the yeast is allowed to finish fermenting. These fermentation tanks are designed to withstand the pressure created as the yeast produces the CO_2 necessary to create the beer's effervescence.

In some commercial mass production breweries this step is bypassed and the fermented brew is injected with CO_2. This process is much faster than "natural" conditioning.

The brew is then bottled, kegged, or, in the case of brewpubs, drawn by taps in the bar, and served to customers.

PREHISTORIC BEER

There is some debate as to whether grain was first cultivated specifically for use in brewing beer or baking bread. However, there is no doubt that the earliest days of "farming" took place back in 8000 B.C., in the Middle East, between the Euphrates and Tigris Rivers. With the desire to form settlements, rather than remaining nomadic and gathering crops where they grew wild, our ancestors developed the practice of agriculture, and civilization was born.

Even before the rise of civilization, the fruits of fermentation were considered gifts from the gods. Wine was probably a happy accident that occured after someone left their fruit juice uncovered for a day or two and noticed the foamy froth that began to appear on the surface of the juice. Then that brave, and lucky, person tasted and enjoyed. It has been suggested that the original beer was discovered when prehistoric man (or woman) let their bowl of grain mush sit for a day or so and sipped the frothy liquid that rose to the surface.

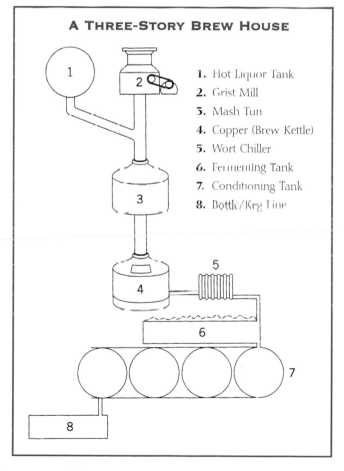

A THREE-STORY BREW HOUSE

1. Hot Liquor Tank
2. Grist Mill
3. Mash Tun
4. Copper (Brew Kettle)
5. Wort Chiller
6. Fermenting Tank
7. Conditioning Tank
8. Bottle/Keg Line

One of the by-products of civilization is the establishment of a complex system of social order. At the top of this social order were the priests. There is little question who got the best of the harvest, as well as the "responsibility" of making sure that wine and beer was made especially to please the gods. Artifacts have been recovered that place beer at the tables of the priests of Ninkasa and Isis.

It was not long before man began to think twice about the idea of reserving beer only for priests or royalty, and not long after that happened, beer became an even more egalitarian beverage.

Ancient texts indicate that after a hard day, the Sumerians, who lived around 3000 B.C., used straws made from reeds to draw off the fermented liquid from special containers of fermented grain and water. This beer played an important part in Sumerian culture, and was consumed by men and women from all social classes. Beer parlors received special mention in the Code of Hammurabi in the eighteenth century B.C.

Stiff penalties were dealt to owners who overcharged customers (death by drowning) or who failed to notify authorities of criminals in their establishments (execution). In the Sumerian and Akkadian dictionaries being studied today, the word for beer is listed in sections relating to medicine, ritual, and myth.

What might this beer have tasted like? The brewers at the Anchor Brewing Company in San Francisco, California were looking for a special event to celebrate the tenth anniversary of their new brew house. They saw an article published by the University Museum of the University of Pennsylvania that described the beer of the ancient Sumerians. Here was their opportunity to brew, literally, a classic. They took up the challenge and, with the help of historians, produced a beer that, according to a member of the staff of the University Museum, "had the smoothness and effervescence of champagne and a slight aroma of dates." Those Sumerians had been on to something good!

When beer found its way to Egypt, it was once again considered a drink fit only for royalty. This beer was made of grain, ginger, and honey, sweetened with date sugar. To lengthen the drinkable "life" of the beer, its alcohol content was raised through the addition of more date sugar.

THE EUROPEAN CONNECTION

As civilization spread north, across the Mediterranean, so did beer. The Greeks called the Egyptian beer a "barley wine," and introduced it to the Romans, who passed it to other civilizations as they traveled through Europe.

Of course, wine is a lot easier to make than beer. All you do is harvest the grapes, crush the juice from them, let that juice ferment, and drink it. The climate of the Mediterranean was, and still is, ideal for growing grapes. Vines were planted specifically for wine production before Greece had conquered the world.

In Northern Europe, where grain grew in abundance, the preference for beer was drawn by agricultural whim. Where grapes grew in abundance, wine was the beverage of choice. Beer and brewing took hold and flourished where grains were a staple for survival. The Mediterranean area produced wine, and the rich breadbasket of Europe became the cradle for the development of beer.

Evidence of the early history of brewing in Europe is meager but reveals that brewing was done by the women as part of maintaining a proper household. The entire family drank fermented beverages made from grain. It was nutritious, and was not nearly as dangerous as drinking the contaminated waters found near most towns and villages. (It must be remembered that what we now consider common sanitary practices were not followed at that time. Potable water was hard to come by in towns because of less-than-efficient human waste disposal. In rural areas ground water was suspect, and spring water was often unavailable.)

MONASTIC BEERS

With the end of the classical Roman and Greek civilizations and the waning of the Holy Roman Empire, the monasteries of Europe were the sole providers of healers, teachers, preachers, and beer. In those times, transportation was by foot, horse, or cart; hence, at its best, travel was tedious and dangerous. In this climate, a tradition of hospitality was practiced by the Roman Catholic monasteries that were way-stations for pilgrims going from one shrine to another, or travelers seeking refuge on a long journey. All visitors were offered refreshment, a place to rest, and a chance to offer prayers and donations for their benefactors. The monks and priests were dedicated to religious pursuits that included humility, poverty, waging wars, the study of nature, illuminating books, and brewing beer as a subsistence beverage. Some religious groups had such strict dietary restrictions that "liquid bread" was the foundation of their existence.

Beer brewed by the members of the religious community was the beverage offered to the visitors. Some monasteries also provided beer for trade, sale, or barter with their neighbors.

At that time, herbs and spices were the pharmacy of those who knew how to unlock their secrets. The "hop" plant was used, for example, as a sedative (in pillows), in shampoo (the oils), and as a leather preservative (resins and oils). The first recorded mention of hops, in relation to brewing, is in the twelfth-century writings of Hildegarde, the Benedictine nun who was abbess of Rupertsberg, near Mainz, Germany. Her writings specifically suggest that hops retard spoilage of beer.

This knowledge was important to every monastery and brewing guild that wanted to expand their markets. For them it was important that the beer they brewed, and shipped, would last the journey intact, and be a credit to their brewing skills. Hops made it possible for beer to endure long trips from the brewery where it was brewed, to the consumer who was paying for a superior product, to what was available as an everyday beverage. (Sounds familiar to the beer mavens of today!)

The growth of cities and the greater use of roads, sea lanes, and caravan routes allowed the beer market to become intercontinental.

KEGS TO GO

In the beginning, beer was brewed for almost immediate consumption by the family or manor folk who brewed it. It was aged for a short while in casks, but not long enough for the wood to impart any significant flavor. If beer was lagered in casks, pitched, lined casks were used.

Of course, there was no real reason to expect a cask of beer to outlast a serving session. The consumption of casks of "cask-conditioned" ale was usually completed by those who opened the cask, in the time it took them to drink the contents.

Once opened, the quality of the beer depended very much on the ability of those present to finish the keg. A beer brewed to almost 12% alcohol by volume, and liberally hopped, could last for, what in those days was, a lifetime!

The next "great leap forward" came with the invention of pasteurization. The process prevented spoilage, and it was easier to control the amount of carbonation when it was "forced " into the beer after pasteurization. Brewers with a "pasteurized" beer needed only to create an extensive distribution network before providing "national" brands. (They also needed a container that made it practical to ship individual servings of a product that was as fresh as it could be.)

BOTTLED BEER

The real beginning of bottled beer dates from the discovery of pasteurization. The Franco-Prussian War, in 1870, had halted the German beer supply to France. In 1875, Louis Pasteur developed a process that would prevent wine and beer from spoiling because of the need to put the French brewing industry on a level with the Germans. Under pressure to keep the home front, and the troops, happy, he carried out experiments which proved that the spoilage of fermented liquids was caused by bacteria. Therefore, yeast free of bacteria produced a fermented beer free of disease. Pasteur found out that by steaming the finished product he could kill all harmful bacteria that cause beer and wine to spoil. This steaming process was soon to become known as *pasteurization*. Pasteurization was done by putting filled, well-corked, bottles into a water bath that was gradually heated (through the use of steam) to 170°F. This heat was sufficient to kill all yeast and bacteria in the solution. It supposedly had little effect on the flavor of the beverage.

Emil Christian Hansen, a Danish biochemist, was to go one step further than Pasteur and prove that certain yeasts, once identified, were harmful in the fermentation process. He worked to produce an absolutely pure culture which would prove best suited for the manufacture of beer.

In November 1883, he produced introduced a pure yeast culture at the Carlsburg Brewery. The discoveries of Pasteur and Hansen are of significant importance in the development of bottled beer.

Many of America's breweries made wide use of these scientific breakthroughs to expand their marketing area. Some of the larger American breweries quickly adopted these discoveries. William J. Uihlein, one of the six brothers who inherited Joseph Schlitz's brewery, brought a pure culture back to America from Copenhagen in 1883. Pabst also adopted the use of pure culture in 1887. Nevertheless, many small breweries in the United States did not take advantage of "modern" technology. They continued to use "family secret" formulas until the advent of Prohibition. Because of this, many small breweries were not able to produce a quality product that could compete with the larger, more scientific breweries.

Bottled beer began to gain favor from the time that brewers were able to produce it in pasteurized form, for it meant the beer could be bottled with the assurance that it would not spoil. Even beer made from bad yeast cultures could be made to last by using the "steaming process."

The glass companies found a friend in Louis Pasteur. Pasteurization required that glass companies produce a strong bottle that could withstand sudden changes in temperatures. Once this was accomplished, great demand was made on the glass companies to produce bottles in exceedingly large numbers, due to the rapid increase in sales of bottled beer.

Adolphus Busch was the first to take advantage of widespread use of bottled beer. He blanketed the country with "The King of Bottled Beer" by the mid-1870s and opened the eyes of the brewing industry. In a short time, after Adolphus Busch proved that beer bottling was economically practical, most other larger breweries followed suit.

What makes the story of bottled beer even more interesting is the curious relationship brewers had with it. At first brewers did not do their own bottling, but set up concessions for those who were willing to do the bottling for them. Those who ran their own bottling department began to call themselves "brewers and bottlers."

Of course, at the time when bottling shops were being established, the U.S. Congress was busy passing laws saying that the bottling of beer could not take place in the brewery, warehouse, or anywhere on brewery premises. (The bottling operation had to be done in a building entirely separated from the brewery.) Casks of beer used in the bottling process had to be carried over the surface of a street or road which was commonly used by the public. This was done so that all the beer produced had to be put in casks or kegs for taxing purposes. All bottled beer had to come from kegs on which the government had already collected tax.

On June 18, 1890, through the efforts of Fred Pabst, the Internal Revenue Act was changed to allow "the construction of pipelines from storage cellars to bottling houses." The bottling house and the brewery still had to remain separate, but the pipeline made bottling much more efficient. The beer was run through a gauge and a tax collector was on hand to see that the appropriate amount of revenue was collected. This method remained in effect until Prohibition.

After Prohibition, the business of "economy of volume" took over. Metal kegs of pressurized beer were the harbingers of doom for the small brewer. Large companies could afford the metal (returnable/reusable with ease) kegs, and fill them with enough beer to keep a bartender busy for a few days. All that was needed was the addition of some extra ingredients to keep the beer looking, and tasting, "fresh" after a long, rough journey from brewer to consumer.

"STYLES" OF BEER AND HOW THEY CAME TO BE

All of the beers brewed before the mid-1800s were essentially what we now call "ales". The only exception to this rule were the "lagers" of southern Germany. Bavarian brewers knew that if they stored their beers in ice-cold caves in the Piedmont of the Alps during the spring and summer months, the resulting beers were smoother and drier than beers that were not lagered. Over time this resulted in the selective survival of the only yeasts that could survive this cold storage–bottom-fermenting (lager) yeast. It was not until 1841 (30 years before Pasteur's work) that the Munich brewer Gabriel Sedlmeyer isolated a strain of bottom-fermenting yeast and began the brewing and fermenting of what we now know as "lager" beer.

To put the idea of different styles in context, it must be remembered that before the industrial revolution most beer was brewed to meet the demands of a family, town, or neighborhood. Beer was consumed because the water, even in rural areas, was not considered potable. The ingredients used to make this beer were from materials close at hand. The local water played a major role in this process. Hard water made the best ales and soft water made the best lagers. Local hops were used, when economical, to add unique flavors. Each strain of hop, having a unique flavor, lent a special character to a local beer. Other ingredients were used to make the basic sweet, alcoholic beer meet the tastes and cuisine of a locality.

It is also important to note that, as today, the cost of the ingredients determined the cost of the finished product. Everyday beer was made from as little malt (sugar) as possible, and was therefore low in alcohol content and relatively inexpensive. A good example of this "style" was called "small beer" and was consumed by the masses in the United Kingdom as a staple beverage.

Local tradition, as well as economy, determined the ratio of roasted malts and various hop varieties that would determine the "style" of a local beverage and its specific flavor characteristics.

HOW MANY STYLES OF BEER ARE THERE?

Although there are only two types of beer (ale and lager), both of these types include a number of styles. Basically there are approximately sixteen styles of beer and ale.

The determination of what constitutes a "style" has been generally codified by brewers and organizations such as the Master Brewers Association of America, Association of Brewers, American Homebrewers Association, CAMRA, and other professional organizations (not to mention beer writers who never miss an opportunity to argue what makes a style legitimate). The following lists these styles, generally from the lightest, most delicate flavored, to the dark, strong-flavored "specialty" brews. The essential difference is determined by the malt, hops, and yeast used in the brewing process. As each chateau has a "signature" that wine connoisseurs can readily detect, certain geographical areas also provide "signature" brews that are just as distinct. The basis for different styles is usually found in the basic ingredients of the brew that are indigenous to a specific area. The other influence is the local cuisine. Brewers are naturally familiar with local cuisine specialties and know that their brews will be expected to enhance favorite foods of their consumers.

It is important that you know the "real thing" when you taste it. It should be similar to the sensual experience of first tasting genuine Roquefort Bleu cheese, or a ripe tomato, fresh off the vine. The Roquefort put all other blue cheeses in context, and that just-picked tomato gave you a different perspective on all those gas-ripened hothouse supermarket tomatos you once paid way too much for.

1. AMERICAN LIGHT LAGER

This style of beer is essentially a pilsner-style lager, brewed with significant quantities of grain other than barley malt; a slightly sweet, lightly hopped, straw-colored, very effervescent beer.

Budweiser

Anheuser-Busch uses nine different hops and special yeast to impart an apple like flavor and aroma to what is really a rather complex beer. Information from the brewer also notes that the grist for Budweiser consists of both two-row and six-row malted barley. (According to the same source, rice is added to impart a dry "snap" to the flavor.)

Beech wood is used in the fermentation process to aid in attenuation. A layer of beech wood chips, cleaned and rinsed before use, is spread on the bottom of the lager tanks to provide more surface area for the action of the yeast.

Alcohol content: 4.8% by volume.

2. PILSNER

This style is a light-straw colored, full-bodied, lagered, bottom-fermented beer named after the town of Pilzen (in what was then known as Bohemia), where it was first brewed in 1842. It quickly became a popular, unique style because it was so different from the amber brews that were the norm at that time.

Pilsner Urquell

Pilsner Urquell (literal translation–"Original from Pilzen"), named for the town of Pilzen, in what is now the Czech Republic, was the first golden-colored lager developed in the seventeenth century. Until that time almost all brews, ale, and lager were amber colored or darker. Pilsner Urquell is, for the most part, still brewed as it was in the late 1800s, when the brewery was refitted with modern nineteenth-century technology.

Today, Pilsner Urquell is brewed with water from the same artesian wells that provided water for the original brewers. The brew has a white head with average size and density, features a golden color, and has a nice malty aroma with subtle spicy undertones.

Alcohol content: 4.8% by volume.

3. BRITISH BITTER

This top-fermented classic ale style offers a deep, rich brown or ruby color with a malty, very lightly hopped flavor. True bitter is only lightly carbonated.

Fuller's London Pride

Fuller's London Pride is the flagship brew of the Fuller's brewery in London. It offers the soft texture, full malt flavor, and honey-flower character of the house yeast. Not a dry-hopped ale, this is a great example of a traditional British "session" beer—one that is meant to be enjoyed, pint after pint, with good friends in a friendly pub.

Alcohol content: 4.1% by volume.

4. PALE ALE

Pale ale, another classic British top-fermented ale style, has more hop flavor than "bitter" but not as much as "India pale ale." (There is a good measure of overlap when other than mainstream examples of these three brew styles are compared.)

Bass

Bass Ale has been brewed in Burton-on-Trent since 1777. The water there, perfect for brewing pale ales, is combined with local barley and hops to create a deep amber-colored brew that was first labeled as pale ale. Bass now carries the appellation "IPA" for India pale ale (although it is no longer brewed specifically to that style). Bass Ale is a classic British pale ale, with good amber color, a malty flavor, and Kent hop for bittering and aroma. The bottled and kegged products are identical except for different carbonation levels. (The bottle has more sparkle.)

Alcohol content: 5% by volume.

5. INDIA PALE ALE

India pale ale, so named because it had to endure long sea voyages from breweries in England to outposts on the fringes of the British empire, had to be a high-gravity, well-hopped brew to enable it to last the voyage and not spoil. Although there are some fine examples still brewed in the United Kingdom, Liberty Ale (brewed in the United States by Anchor Brewing Company, San Francisco) is a particularly well-balanced brew.

Anchor Liberty Ale

Liberty Ale was released in 1975 as Anchor's original Christmas beer. It is a top-fermented ale, naturally carbonated, and dry-hopped for a very floral aroma, and dry flavor.

Alcohol content: Not available.

6. VIENNA LAGER

This was once the style "à la mode" in Vienna at the turn of the nineteenth century. Then it fell from fashion and left Europe for the warmer climate of Mexico. Today, the only true "Vienna" lager is Dos Equis, but with the growth of the specialty beer market it may not hold its special place for long.

Dos Equis

The unique, almost red, color and roasted malt flavor of Dos Equis is the result of the judicious use of special crystal malt (a malt that is roasted before it has dried after sprouting gives a unique color and flavor to the beer), and roasted malt. Traditional hops and special water treatments result in a beer, from Mexico, that is a good example of the color and flavor of what was once a popular style of beer brewed, almost exclusively, in Vienna, Austria.

Alcohol content: 4.7% by volume.

7. BROWN ALE

Brown ale is a traditional British, top-fermented ale. Flavor and color are very much like a pale ale, but sweeter and darker.

Newcastle Brown Ale

Newcastle Brown Ale was created in Newcastle upon Tyne in the northeast of England during the 1920s. Distinct in color, it has a nutlike flavor and a fine head. It is sold in the United States in 12-ounce bottles, British "pint" bottles, and on draft.

Alcohol content: 4.7% by volume.

8. SCOTTISH ALE

This is a strong (high-alcohol) brew made with Scottish malted barley. Less hoppy than English brews, there are hints of caramel and, sometimes, a slight tang of smoke in the flavor.

McEwan's Scotch Ale

The William McEwan brewery, founded in 1856, merged with the William Younger brewery to form the Scottish Brewers in 1931. In 1960, it underwent another incarnation and became part of Scottish & Newcastle. Today, the McEwan's Scotch Ale is still brewed at McEwan's Fountain Brewery in Edinburgh, Scotland.

McEwan's Scotch Ale is strong, rich, and very dark brown in appearance; not quite opaque. Its aroma is a combination of malt and alcohol, with a slight roast tinge. In the mouth, the beer is full-bodied, smooth, and malty sweet. In the finish, the sweetness is offset by a hint of roastiness.

Alcohol content: 5.1% by volume

9. STRONG ALE

Also called "old ale", this strong (high-alcohol) brew is particular for its dark color (almost opaque) and a very sweet flavor that masks the heat of an alcohol content that can reach 6–8% by volume.

Theakston's Old Peculier

No, the brewmaster was not tippling when he spelled the name of this beer. *Webster's Unabridged* defines a *peculier* as "a church or parish exempt from the jurisdiction of the ordinary in whose territory it lies." (An ordinary, of course, being "a prelate exercising actual ecclesiastical jurisdiction over a specified territory.") Graced with the seal of the official of the peculier of Masham on its label, the name "Old Peculier" finally makes sense.

This rather special brew, made from pale ale and crystal malts, wheat, caramel, and three types of sugar, is a very high gravity beer. Fuggles is the most prevalent hop used, but it is used in concert with Northern Brewer for balance. The yeast is a mixed strain, rather than pure culture. This has helped it endure for over 30 years.

Theakston's Old Peculier is imported into the United States by Scottish & Newcastle. The product is sold only in bottles in the United States. Those lucky enough to travel to Yorkshire and sample this beer from the cask will truly have an experience they will want to tell their grandchildren about.

Alcohol content: 6-8% by volume.

10. BARLEYWINE

Barleywine is a very dark, almost opaque ale. The term "barleywine" is a fairly new term. Once called "strong ale," this is the most alcoholic style of beer. The addition of a healthy amount of hops forms a powerful flavor triad of sweet malt, bitter hops, and warm alcohol. Alcohol content can reach 10% by volume.

Anchor Old Foghorn

First brewed in 1975, Old Foghorn Barleywine became available year-round in 1985. Brewed in small batches, to maintain an extremely high original gravity, Old Foghorn is top-fermented and dry-hopped. Although there are other barleywines brewed in the United States and the United Kingdom, this particular beer is packed to the gunwales with hops, yet manages to balance a body of almost epic proportions and high alcohol content fit for a seadog.

Alcohol content: Not available.

11. BOCK BEER

This style is similar to strong ale but it is fermented with bottom-fermenting yeast and is "lagered" (aged) for at least a month. This is truly a "substantial" beer, as is noted in the following profile.

Paulaner Salvator

Italian monks from the order of St. Francis, invited to Munich in 1624 during the Counter-Reformation period, led a very strict existence. Their religious beliefs forbid the consumption of meat, butter, milk, and eggs, and allowed only fish, bread, vegetables, and vegetarian liquids. In order to supplement their poor nutrition, the Paulaner Monks learned to brew a special beer. In 1627, Father Barnabas began brewing a dark beer rich in nutrients necessary for the continued survival of his order.

When the monks got permission from the local court to sell their beer to the local population in 1780, they produced a doppel bock (this is a beer similar to barleywine except that it is fermented with bottom-fermenting yeast) which, they called Salvator (pronounced sal-VA-tor). This was the mother of double bocks. Other double bocks put "-ator" at the end of their name in honor of this fine brew.

The tradition is commemorated with the depiction, on the label, of Father Barnabas presenting a mug of Salvator to the Duke of Bavaria.

Alcohol content: 7.5% by volume.

12. PORTER

It was a sad fact that the "porter" of Charles Dickens' time is gone. The day when porter "died" funeral processions were held in the United Kingdom to mark the event. There are some alive now who remember that day. Although the specific yeast is not used any more, the style lives on in the United States where there are brewers who will not give up the ghost. Although there are a number of microbreweries now producing porter-style beers, they must, through default, compare themselves to "The Celebrated Pottsville Porter."

Yeungling Porter

For those in the know, this is a real "sleeper." Brewed in Pottsville, Pennsylvania since 1914, this is a dry, roasty brew that is darker than amber and lighter than "stout." Yeungling has the malt for its porter specially roasted to give it a unique flavor.

Alcohol content: 5% by volume.

13. STOUT

Although there are many stouts brewed both in the United States and the Republic of Ireland, Guinness Stout is perceived as the touchstone for all stouts. To ensure quality control, Guinness roasts malt specifically for their own production needs.

Guinness Stout

All the grain used by Guinness is grown in Ireland. The assortment of roasted malts is complemented by the addition of 25% flaked barley and 10% roasted barley. The hops are mostly Kent Goldings, and fermentation is done with a strain of its original yeast, which was isolated in the early 1960s. The yeast works at high temperatures (around 77°F/25°C).

Alcohol content: 4.8% by volume.

14. WHEAT BEER

Wheat beer, with usually 30% wheat added to the grist, and brewed with a special yeast, is especially popular in Bavaria. It is also a major style of beer brewed in Belgium. Wheat beer has a distinctive sour flavor and, in the case of Bavarian wheat beers, a unique flavor of clove. The distinctive flavor is due mainly to the flavors created by the special yeast during fermentation.

Paulaner Hefe–Weizen

Paulaner Hefe-Weizen starts with a two-mash process using dark- and light-colored brewing malt from two-row Bavarian summer barley; dark- and light-colored malted wheat, and caramelized malt. This top-fermented beer contains more than half wheat. Hallertau hops are used for both bittering and aroma. Lager yeast is used and the beer is allowed to lager for approximately 2–3 weeks at –1°C.

Alcohol content: 5.5% by volume.

15. BELGIAN STYLES

Belgian beers are a style unto themselves because of the unique characteristics that are given to the beers by the unique yeasts that are allowed to ferment them.

(a) Flanders Red Ales: Rodenbach

Among the "red beers," Rodenbach is considered the quintessential example of the style. Visitors to the brewery in Roeselaere can see the 300 oak casks (the brewery has four coopers to maintain tuns), all more than 20 feet high, where the beer is aged. Rodenbach is brewed from four malts, one pale from summer barley, two- and six-row varieties of winter malted barley, and crystal (Vienna) roasted malt. The hops are mainly Brewers Gold, with some Kent Goldings. Five different strains of yeast are used in the fermentation process.

Alcohol content: 4.6% by volume.

(b) Lambic: Lindeman's Kriek

Lindeman's Kriek is a top-fermented cherry-flavored lambic (70% malted barley and 30% unmalted wheat) with a rose color. It has an aroma of cherries and is very sparkling, refreshing with a dry finish. The acidic flavor of the lambic blends well with the cherry flavor. This beer is best served in a champagne flute at 45°F. It is sold in 750-ml bottles.

Alcohol content: Not available.

Lindeman's Gueuze

Gueuze, possibly the oldest beer style, is unseasoned wheat beer, fermented with the ambient yeast from the region in, and around, Brussels. It is prized by beer lovers who "lay it down" in a cool, dark place, like fine wine.

Lindemans Gueuze is golden-colored, with a cidery, winelike flavor. It is similar, in flavor profile, to a sparkling vermouth.

Alcohol content: 6.1% by volume.

Liefman's Frambozenbier

Most Belgian frambozenbier are made from lambic beers infused with fruit. The Liefman's Frambozenbier is made from a base of Goudenband Brown Ale. This beer was introduced in Belgium in October 1985.

The main flavor is the winelike essence of the brown ale. The raspberry flavor quickly becomes evident and the finish is sharp and refreshing. This is a very effervescent beverage, even more lively than the weiss beers of Munich.

This beer should be stored, and served, just slightly chilled to fully appreciate the aroma of the raspberries and the flavor of the ale.

Alcohol content: 5.0% by volume

(c) Belgian Strong: Duvel

Duvel is brewed by the Moorgat brewery in Breendonk, in Belgium. It is regarded as the quintessential pale strong ale, with a flavor that is complex and deep. It is made with Danish summer barley malt, whole flower Styrian and Saaz hops. Duvel undergoes three fermentations. The first is warm, the second cold, and the final one takes place in the bottle, lasting 5 weeks.

Alcohol content: 8.5 by volume.

(d) Trappist: Chimay

Chimay (pronounced "she-may") produces three types of Trappist beers, identified by the color of the metal cap that tops their distinctive cork-finished bottles: Premier Chimay (red), Cinq Cents (white), and Grand Reserve (blue). The red, as well as the blue, has a very particular "house character" that is fruity and sweetish, with a soft, full, deep body. The beer is dark brown with a ruby hue. The white Chimay is much hoppier and drier, with a quenching hint of acidity. It also has a paler color, more amber than ruby red.

Alcohol content: Premier Chimay (red), 7% by volume.
Cinq Cents (white): 8% by volume.
Grand Reserve (blue): 9% by volume.

16. SPECIALTY BEERS

These unique beers do not easily fit into any particular style. Each is considered to stand alone as a special beer.

(a) Steam Beer

Today, "Steam Beer" is a trademark of the Anchor Brewing Company of San Francisco, California. In the nineteenth century steam beer was a nickname for local beers that were fermented with lager yeast, at ale yeast temperature, producing beers with alelike character. It may also have been common practice to "top off" kegs of beer with beer that had not finished its first fermentation. The result was an in-keg fermentation that produced high levels of natural carbonation. With no refrigeration to control this fermentation, a freshly tapped keg would produce copious amounts of foam or "steam."

Anchor Steam Beer

Anchor Steam Beer is the standard of a style of hoppy, malty beer. It has the crisp flavor features of a lager, and the esters (fruitiness), complex aromas, and flavor base of an ale. Dark amber in color, the grist is American grown malt (pale and roasted) and hops are from the American Northwest.

Alcohol content: Not available.

(b) Herbed/Spiced: Anchor Our Special Ale

Every year since 1975, Anchor has brewed a Christmas ale. It is produced in small quantities and is available only from late November until early January. Each year the recipe is changed and there is a special label designed around the tree, a traditional symbol of renewal. Properly refrigerated, this beer remains drinkable for years.

Alcohol content: Not available.

(c) Smoked Beer: Kaiserdom Rauchbier

Kaiserdom is brewed in Bamberg, Germany. It is brewed from malt that has been smoked in a way similar to the process of smoking malted barley in the making of Scotch whiskey. The technique of smoking malted barley to dry it and add color was used before the more modern method of indirect kilning was introduced.

Kaiserdom Rauchbier is brewed from Bavarian barley that has been roasted over a fire of moist beechwood logs. Whole Hallertau hops are used to provide flavor and aroma. The fermentation is a bottom fermentation, and the beer is lagered for 3 months. The finished product is a beer of conventional alcohol content, with a dark color and complex smoky flavor characteristics.

Alcohol content: 4.2% by weight

(d) Strong Lager: Samichlaus Bier

Brewed just one day a year, on December 6th (St. Nicholas Day in Switzerland), Samichlaus is aged for 10 months before bottling for the American market. The beer is bottled for a full year in Switzerland. Samichlaus is brewed with two-row summer barley malt (Pilsner and Munich styles), two varieties of Hallertau hops, and special yeast that can metabolize in a high alcohol environment. Samichlaus begins with 3 pounds of dissolved solids in each gallon of wort (weighing 10 pounds) and after fermentation there is still 1/4 of a pound of unfermented solids in each gallon of finished beer. Although it is a lager, this beer should be stored and served at cellar temperature (50°F) in order to fully appreciate its flavor and aroma. Samichlaus has been called "the world's strongest lager" by many beer experts.

Alcohol content. 14.9% by volume

(e) Oktoberfest: Paulaner Oktoberfest Marzen

Traditionally, when the last of each winter season's beer was brewed, in March, it was made a little stronger than usual, so that the alcohol content would preserve it through the summer. By then the beer was very well attenuated and sporting a relatively high alcohol content. Today that tradition continues with the brewing of Marzen, or "March Beer."

Paulaner Marzen starts with a two-mash process using dark- and light-colored brewing malt from two-row Bavarian summer barley. Hallertau hops are used for both bittering and aroma. Lager yeast is used and the beer is allowed to lager for approximately 4 weeks at –1°C.

Alcohol content: 5% by volume.

CHAPTER 2

Cooking with Beer

The recent growth of the microbreweries and brewpubs has caught the attention of chefs and restaurateurs in the same way California wines caught their attention 20 years ago. When the first boutique wineries took root in the Napa, Russian River, and Carnaros regions in the 1970s, the ideal was to develop wines similar to the best of the European wines. What happened was the development of wines that were very different from their European cousins but with just as interesting and complex a flavor.

Today, breweries in the United States and Canada are producing brews based on every distinctive style of beer known in the world. The range of flavors goes from an ethereal, straw-colored lager with just a whisper of hops, to deep garnet-colored pale ales with enough hops to dry up an ocean. These beers, and their range of flavors, challenge the culinary skills of beer lovers, gourmets, and professional chefs like nothing else that has appeared on the scene in a long time.

Although there are similarities between using beer and using wine in the kitchen, there are some major differences as well. The unique flavor of hops offers the interested cook a chance to stretch his or her culinary imagination and sense of taste. The sweet grain flavor of malt offers its own accent to shimmering soups, stout stews, and braised beef dishes. Special surprises await those who have a weakness for desserts.

The first people to extensively use fresh, rich, flavorful craft-brewed beers in their kitchens were the brave souls who ran the kitchens of the first brewpubs. Although beer is the featured attraction at a brewpub, the effort to ensure the quality of the beer should be matched by an effort to ensure the quality of the food served. To do this, many owners of long-established brewpubs have professional brewmasters in their brew house, and professional chefs running their kitchen.

Brewpubs that are more than 3 years old (rumored to be the life expectancy of a restaurant) have succeeded because they could deliver consistently good food as well as consistently good beer. This has taken a lot of trial and error as well as imaginative solutions when it came to balancing the unique characteristics of the house brew to the particular characteristics of the food served.

In this section we will hear from chefs who are using beer as an important ingredient in their kitchens. From the wildly enthusiastic, to the cautiously interested, each of the following chefs has a unique insight or observation that helps put the concept of cooking with beer in context with more traditional cooking techniques.

One of the more interesting brewery-restaurants in the Boston area is John Harvard's. Here, the menu is extensive rather than spare. The beers are brewed to the style of British ales and imaginative specialty beers.

Joe Kubic, with the business from the beginning, has developed his menu with a solid understanding of what makes up the flavors of the many styles of beer. Combined with a classic culinary background, the excitement he feels about where beer and food pairings are going is evident in the following collection of Chef Kubik's thoughts.

JOE KUBIK

JOHN HARVARD'S, CAMBRIDGE, MA

When I interviewed for the job of chef at John Harvard's they explained to me that they were going to open a "brewery-restaurant." I was told that they had been to about 80 of them so far and, although the beer was good, they had not found any where the food matched the quality of the beer. What they wanted was good food with honest beer. That sounded good to me. I wanted to be on the cutting edge of what was happening.

I can't say that I was very interested in beer before I started working here at John Harvard's. I remember when I was working at the Carlyle Hotel in Manhattan in 1980, it was all classic French cuisine and everything came out of Le Repertoire…there was a lot of French spoken—it was all French….We did a classic braised beef dish that called for a combination of half beer and half white wine. The first time I made that big reduction with the beer in the sauce, that's when I learned why they used half wine and half beer. At the time I thought that they used half beer to get the taste of the beer. Now I know that the wine smoothes out the bitter accents of the hops and the hops accent the dryness of the white wine.

Having spent a lot of time in French kitchens, and understanding the different wines and their results in reductions, I would make a red wine sauce with a good burgundy and finish it with beer. That way I got the complex flavors without letting one or the other become overpowering. I learned, a long time ago, that a sauce accompanies a dish and doesn't overpower it. It isn't the prevalent appeal of the dish. When you taste the red wine sauce it is not that you are tasting a Beaujolais, or Burgundy, or a good red wine—you are tasting other things as well. When you make a sauce with beer it is always better to finish the sauce with beer as opposed to starting with it in a reduction, because the hops could be concentrated and the sauce would get too bitter and overpower the food. When you make a sauce and finish it with beer, the malt and hop aromas seem to hover over the sauce. That is why I never add the beer until the last moment. This way I can ensure that the sauce gets such a fresh flavor and the aroma of malt and hops that the essence of the beer seems to just hover above the sauce. You can really pick up a nice flavor by dropping a little Nut Brown Ale or a little Stout into a standard red wine reduction. It really adds something unique to the sauce.

It wasn't until about 3 or 4 months after we opened that I really had an opportunity to spend a good deal of time and learn a lot more about our beer from our brewmaster Tim Morse. He's the one, when sitting in the office talking one night, who taught me about the flavor components of beer. I'll never forget some of the things he told me. I learned that malt is the "soul" of beer and the hops are the "spice" of beer. That got me thinking about doing a barley malt and Ceylon Tea sorbet. ... We had already decided to do some beer dinners and the sorbet was an ideal intermezzo between courses when the brewer wanted to talk about the wort. So I worked out a recipe with his wort and added the Ceylon tea to it, we bought an ice cream maker and produced our sorbet for the first beer dinner. It is now regularly featured on the menu.

At John Harvard's we produce all of our sausage in-house. When I learned more about hops I started to use them when smoking some of our foods. It was for a recent beer dinner that we added some hops to the wood we were using to smoke a venison salami. It came out almost too perfect. We have also used Cascade hops as an extra touch when we smoked our own salmon to get a little citric or minty aroma onto the salmon. I decided to do a maple-smoked salmon and used some apples, salt, and maple syrup to marinate the salmon. Then I used some maplewood for the smoke. I used a very small amount of Cascade hops that gave the salmon a cool, minty dimension.

DAVID PAGE

HOME RESTAURANT, NEW YORK, NY

"Beer was always something served at the table in my family" says Chef David Page. With his pony tail, baseball cap, and intense gaze, Chef Page gives the appearance of a lanky young man just in from fixing a mower or checking on the livestock in the north pasture.

His restaurant, Home, is a long, thin space with a soft gold, almost amber ambiance. The atmosphere is that of a country bed & breakfast.

My family always used beer in traditional Wisconsin "hearty food." Bratwursts in beer, etc.... We didn't think about it when we used it. Now I actually have to stop and think about it and explain why I use it.

There is also a romantic quality to a meal like **Venison Sausage, Boston Brown Bread** and **Baked Cranberry Beans** that almost everyone can appreciate.

To use the term "brewpub" to describe the Big River Grille & Brewing Works would be misleading. The progress of this organization has been followed for the last year or so, with much interest, by all of the major foodservice trade publications and stock analysts. Their arrangement with the Rock Bottom Brewery organization brought the growth potential of brewery-restaurants to the attention of the restaurant industry. And then Big River was awarded the contract to operate the first brewery-restaurant in DisneyWorld™ in Florida. You can find that Big River at the new Disney "Boardwalk" resort.

The question remains: Can a large operation present diners with the same imaginative offerings presented by much smaller, more intimate pub-style restaurants? So far, the key to their success has been attention to quality and detail. Chef Richard Hamilton learned about beer at the source, wandering through Europe. Today he finds himself baking with beer. This is how he told it to me.

CORPORATE CHEF RICHARD HAMILTON
BIG RIVER GRILLE & BREWING WORKS, Chattanooga, TN

When I lived in Europe I was always trying different types of beers. There were the raspberry beers, peach beers, lager beers, stout beers. I enjoyed discovering the different flavors. If you are going to use a beer in a dish, the flavor should come out and you should be able to know that there is a beer in it. If you are going to have a dish of asparagus with a beer sauce on it, I want to taste the beer in that sauce.

There is not much in the Escoffier training that teaches about using beer in cooking traditional French cuisine; however, the chefs who taught me tended to push me into trying different things. Since there is no ingredient flavor in beer that you don't already use in food preparation, the process of substituting beer for a specific flavor or effect is relatively simple, if you pay attention to what you are doing. For example, I use beer in my bread rolls because beer has yeast in it and it has sugar in it. All I have to figure out is how to practically replace the yeast and the other sugars in the traditional recipe.

A lot of people would try to overthink it and make it more complicated than it is. The challenge of working with the bitter accents of hops in beer. … The bitterness of the beer makes it very important that you pair it with the right thing. The beer [flavor] has got to come out, but if you use it in a shrimp dish in a batter, I don't want the beer to be so strong that you cannot taste the shrimp.

So finding the right combination is just like finding the right wine to use in a dish. you are not going to put a white wine in a game dish because you would lose all the subtlety of the wine's flavors. At the same time you wouldn't put a super heavy stout on a crab dish or another delicate-flavored dish.

The key is to experiment, to do the same dish in many different ways. Taste the beer and taste the food that you want to try using the beer with. Get a good understanding of what you are dealing with. Whenever I sit down and try to come up with recipes, I first taste the beer and try to envision what flavors do in my mouth, and what would go with those flavors. Sometimes it works and sometimes it doesn't. There are no hard and fast rules to using beer in food.

Certain flavors, when you get them in your mouth, evoke certain feelings in you. You taste a nice hot chili and you might recall the feeling of winter, and the comfort of an open fire in a fireplace. Flavors are very much comfort feelings for people. When you prepare food, part of the whole experience of eating is to be able to bring those feelings out. It is important to carry those feelings over into the food.

Chef (call me Rick) Moonen is the chef/co-owner of Oceana, a fine-dining seafood restaurant in Manhattan. He is also well known as a "beer-chef" by his fellow food professionals. He has been using beer in his kitchens for over 10 years. While working at the Water Club, a fine-dining restaurant in New York, he and a few friends, also chefs, ran a place called Chefs and Cuisinaires Club, or CCC for short. This was a place where, after working a long day in a kitchen, a group of food professionals could get together for a dish or two, a beer or two, and some good conversation among friends. The menu was always very "beer friendly" to complement a choice beer list that included a few excellent beers on draft, and a good number of interesting bottled beers. Moonen was always looking for the most interesting beers to serve at CCC. A number of breweries, knowing the place was a hangout for chefs, would arrange to have samples of their best products find their way there.

RICK MOONEN

OCEANA, NEW YORK, NY

I attended the Culinary Institute of America and graduated in 1978. While I was there I met a Belgian chef who taught me a good deal about the classic Belgian dishes that, naturally, use beer as a basic ingredient. Not only did I learn the dishes, I also discovered many of the unique beers that come from Belgium.

I found out about the world of unique beers in this country on a visit to the Anchor Brewing Company in San Francisco. Dr. Joe Owades was giving a 3-day seminar on beer that was very intensive. I was there at 4:00 AM with steel-toed brewers' boots on and ready to learn how beer is brewed. That was some day! I worked on the beer from shoveling malt into the grist mill, to shoveling the spent grain from the mash tun.

They taught me about the different malts and hops they used. It was a great way to discover the flavors and aromas that all go into making beer. Since then I have been very interested in the development of the craft breweries and the brewery-restaurants that are springing up all over the United States.

Recently Chef Moonen moved uptown to become chef/co-owner of Oceana, a fine-dining restaurant with a menu that features fish and shellfish in good numbers. Although there is a fine wine list available, beer still plays a role. Of particular interest is the selection of fresh oysters used in a number of appetizers at Oceana. A delicate fresh Malpeque, set atop a slender glass filled with crushed ice, or six succulent oysters served in a bamboo steamer, are served with St. Christoffel, a crisp Dutch lager. That particular beer complements the salinity of the oyster and refreshes the pallet for the next taste treat. At Oceana that might mean a touch of caviar. Chef Moonen is first to admit that he is especially partial to beer and caviar.

A good example of how beer works with stronger tasting food is pairing beer and caviar. A good dry pilsner beer with caviar is a perfect match. The traditional match of caviar and champagne is really overkill. Many people find the "fishy" flavor of the caviar is not a good match with the acid of the champagne. A pilsner, on the other hand, is a dry and slightly bitter flavor that matches the "sea" flavor of caviar. In fact, it goes well with anything that is salty or a little oily.

A Spaten or dry lager like a Pilsner Urquel would be perfect with caviar or smoked salmon. Let the experts pour champagne; just pour a nice crisp pilsner in a flute and enjoy!

CHEF STEVE LYLE

ODEON, NEW YORK, NY

The Odeon could have been used as a bistro set in one of Jean-Paul Belmondo's black-and-white film noirs produced in the late 1950s. There is a comfortable contrast between the molasses-brown wood fixtures and paneling against the parchment-brown walls that creates a relaxing ambiance.

Business was slow on the humid, rainy afternoon when I met the chef, Steve Lyle. As we introduced ourselves, only two tables were occupied. At one sat Spike Lee deep in conversation with his associate. The other table accommodated a man and woman, both in traditional business suits. They were intently sharing a bottle of sparkling water and a yellow legal notepad.

The variables are endless compared to working with wine. Most important to keep in mind is to use common sense. I don't think that the mass-marketed American beers have the variety of styles to compete with the variety of styles found in Europe. They lack the depth, crispness, and structure of the European beers.

Good beer is something that improves the enjoyability of most dishes. With the "craft beers" there is the perception that these are a "cut above" the kind of thing you drink for effect. I enjoy Warsteiner because it is a refreshingly dry beer that can be quaffed. Other beers that I like to enjoy, in a more leisurely manner,

are the line of beers from the Dock Street and Harpoon Brewing companies, also
Celis White.

Yes I do have one or two dishes I use beer in. Sometimes, when I have a
special soup, I find that beer "bites up" the soup when you splash some in at the
last minute. The dry hop flavor makes a very interesting finishing flavor.

I also have a dish of Duck Legs Braised with Onions in Brooklyn Brown Ale
on the menu. There is a richness to the beer in the sauce that balances nicely
with the sweetness of the almost caramelized onions and the rich, almost gami-
ness of the duck. As I'm talking about these flavors I'm thinking it might be interesting to try the same dish with Catamount Pale Ale....

For every chef who is just getting interested in beer and cooking, there is
another who is taking the "beer explosion" in stride. For them, beer is just another taste sensation to use when developing new dishes or re-thinking traditional
dishes. For these chefs it is a matter of getting down to basics.

CHEF SEAN WOODS
RITZ CARLTON ON AMELIA ISLAND, AMELIA ISLAND, FL

I don't have any problem cooking with beers, as long as you keep your
basic cooking fundamentals involved. I cook with a lot of spirits and I use
beer just like I would use them and it doesn't create any problem. It is
just like any other ingredient, as long as you follow the basic principles.
Have a method in mind and an outcome that you want to achieve—
what you are trying to get out of the beer and what kind of flavor
you are looking for.

Now at the Rainbow Room in New York City, Chef Waldy
Malouf had begun to explore the flavors of New York State craft beers
while at the Hudson River Club in the World Financial Center, where the theme was
to highlight the produce of New York State. Chef Malouf recalls how he first discovered how interesting beer can be.

CHEF WALDY MALOUF
HUDSON RIVER CLUB, NEW YORK, NY

Ten years ago I was working at a French restaurant in Westchester, New York.
They had a small selection of European beers on the menu. I was surprised to
find how different these beers tasted compared to mainstream commercial beers.
Flavors are piqued when you pour beer instead of wines.

Then the owners expanded their inventory to include Belgian and Alsatian
beers. In a fine-dining restaurant I had never seen beer presented as an alterna-

tive to wine. It was interesting to begin to see where beers fit into that kind of cuisine. When I was there I also cooked with some beans, mainly carbonnades and stews....

The only problem I found was in using beers in reductions. A thick reduction can make a major change in the flavors. Once you know that, it isn't difficult to work with beers. It's a matter of "simmer, but don't reduce."

One of my favorite recipes using beer is an acorn/butternut squash soup finished with pale ale. It is very popular with my customers and fun to work with. The squash is sweet and the beer "lifts" the soup's texture...keeps it carbonated and results in a "whipped effect."

Personally, I like to have fun with the bitter flavors in beer, especially a hoppy pilsner with chocolate or dried fruit. With dried fruit the sugar is concentrated and intense. I'll let you in on my secret passion—a cool lager and Raisinettes™...a hoppy ale and steamed chocolate pudding with raisins...Indian pudding....

Now that I have become more interested in beer, the first thing I try when I visit a new country is the local beer. Surprisingly I have found some very nice beers in the Middle East...Egypt has excellent local beers.

Local beers and local produce might have been the theme at the Hudson River Club, but the whole range of regional foods found in the United States was the inspiration for the owners of Heartland Brewery, also in New York City.

CHEF ANDREW LASSETER

HEARTLAND BREWERY, NEW YORK, NY

April in New York City can be sparkling. It was on one such Wednesday morning that I met Chef Andrew Lasseter and owner/brewmaster Jim Migliorini at their brewery/restaurant called Heartland Brewery. Located just across the street from Union Square Park, there is always an immediate sense of the slowly changing seasons as leaves turn from bright green to deep green in the summer, only to toast to red, brown, and auburn under the last glowing rays of the summer sun, and falling to the ground leaving the trees to sleep through another icy city winter. It is fitting that the changes of the calendar are also marked by the seasonal changes in the styles of beer brewed here.

Each season has a beer that is peculiar to it because each season calls for a different flavor to toast the passing of time. Spring is impatient and effervescent as a fresh hefe-weizen just poured into the traditional tall glass. Summer is a lazy glass of lager on a hot afternoon that is mellowing into the rich autumnal flavors of ales and porters. Finally, there is winter chill to banish with brews such as barleywine.

Less potent, but certainly flavorful, are the spiced ales now being made popular by regional breweries, and marketed as "Christmas" or "Holiday" brew.

It was, as I said, a fine spring day. In the sunlit front room at Heartland, we talked about beer, and food.

Chef Lassiter and Jim Migliorini both began by commenting on their shared philosophy of what they were trying to do with the cuisine, brewing selections, and ambiance at Heartland.

We are looking to the flavors of traditional regional dishes here in the United States to go with our line of fresh beer…Our interest in using things grown and marketed here in the United States is even part of our brewing philosophy. We use only malt, hops, and roasted grains from the farms here in the United States.

The theme of local flavors has also been an inspiration for other chefs. Don Sullivan grew up on the North Shore of Long Island. This area was, and still is, a place of farms, fishermen, and wineries. Chef Sullivan, who only recently opened the Southampton Publick House, first discovered his appreciation of beer when he decided to "help out" a friend who was going to open a steak house in the rather desolate section known as the Flatiron District of Manhattan, a few years ago. In the late fall, and certainly in the winter, the south shore of Long Island also seems to be a rather desolate place. This is when the summer houses are shuttered and populations of many small towns can drop by a third. Nevertheless, there are many who live and work in this region known for farms, potatoes, and a population of what are called "Baymen." These are the fishermen who work the local waters, the local oyster and clam beds in particular.

When the Southampton Publick House was opened, the menu featured local produce, almost exclusively. Chef Don Sullivan and brewmaster Phil Markowsky focused on the available local produce and present a selection of beers and a menu of dishes that are both seasonal and focused on the unique local produce, especially from the sea. When I asked Chef Sullivan for a recipe, he almost instantly thought of his **Baymen's Pie**, a rustic savory pie (we chatted in late autumn) with the sea-salt tang of oysters. The thought of a slice of this pie, and a cool glass of stout, on a brisk November afternoon, is more than enough to tempt one out to the South Shore of Long Island.

CHEF DON SULLIVAN
SOUTHAMPTON PUBLICK HOUSE, SOUTHAMPTON, NY

While I went to school I was also a full-time chef running the kitchen at a new place called J. P. Laughlin's New York Grill. This was really one of the pioneer restaurants in the Flatiron District, which has now become one of the hottest areas in the city. Jimmy Laughlin and I were friends from the East End of Long Island and I had just entered in the program in September at NYU. What started as a weekend to help him set up turned into a 2-year full-time job and it was doing great. I lived in the neighborhood and walked to school and to work.

Jimmy was a big beer lover. He opened a classic New York grill and his idea was to offer steaks and chops and international beers. He had things that I had never seen before, being the Budweiser, Coors, Heineken drinker that I was. He had Peroni, Tsing Tao, beers that you wouldn't normally find at the big stores or distributors back then. They were the classic English ales and the German lagers…. He rotated them. That was what got me interested in beers, learning all the different beers that were available, even back then.

We opened J. P. Laughlin's New York Grill in September 1986. Jimmy was one of the first to bring steaks back and one of the first to begin featuring an extensive line of beers. He had 50-plus beers lined up in bottles behind the bar, which really worked as a great selling point, plus he had eight taps going. Little did he and I know that we had hit on a niche of people who were getting into beer. The East Village for many years had a couple of bars that were beer bars, so we got a lot of that crowd, and it didn't hurt having 24-ounce steaks and babyback ribs, roasts, and what not.

Then I got involved with the people who opened the Yorkville Brewery in Manhattan. I had a restaurant called Riptides out in the Hamptons and we were seasonal, opened March through October, so I got involved with them. They were acquaintances, friends, and we were able to do a lot of the same things that I did at New York Grill. There was a mutual relationship there also…I brought beer-influenced recipes and more of a lighter fare than what we had at Laughlin's. He was really into being a brewpub at Yorkville and that was more burger-oriented…more pub-oriented than restaurant-oriented. That was what impressed me and I saw that the beer and food connection was going to snowball and become something big.

Then this location came into play and it is an amazing location. Publick House has an 80-year history of being an inn-tavern-restaurant. It is an exceptionally remarkable building from an architectural standpoint in the heart of Southampton Village. It is like a natural for us because the building lends itself to year-round personality, so we were confident that the microbrewery, hand-crafted ale movement, so to speak, would allow us to be year-round here. Also, the beer really lends itself to the cooler seasons. In the summertime you have your seasonal population, but in the winter it's also beautiful out here; we also have made a conscious effort to tie in with the harvest season.

What most people don't realize is that the area is very heavily farm-oriented, which is a perfect relationship with the beer. We have year-round seafood which is the best in the world, along with seasonal produce from nearby farms—some of the best on the East coast on the South Fork, and we also have a perfect tie-in with the local vineyards. Long Island has about 15 or 16 wineries that are widely regarded now,—20 years after the vineyard movement started out here,   as quality wine producers. We like to highlight those wines here. We have also entered into a partnership with the oldest ranch in America, the Deep Hollow Ranch in Montauk. They pick up all of our spent grain, and their livestock was transferred over from the processed feed so there is an obvious savings in us not having to dispose of the spent grain in a landfill. Obviously the ranch is getting about 2,000 pounds of grain a week free of charge and he is very environmentally active out here

We have put a lot of thought and attention to detail here at the Publick House regarding how the restaurant is perceived. We present ourselves as a restaurant that houses a brewery and makes its own beer. We feel that in terms of stressing quality of product and quality of service, not only for the beer, which we feels speaks for itself, but in having Phil Markowsky as part of our team. We did the same for the facility. We renovated a one hundred year old building and it looks sharp. The food needs to be the same—we use all local shellfish. We use about 90% local fish and the 10% is salmon or gulf fish.

In terms of regional fish, the striped bass are running now offshore, so that is on the menu. Ten years ago you couldn't get striped bass, five years ago you couldn't get striped bass because of the pollution. Oysters go beautifully with our porter, the classic English combination. So there are a lot of small details.

When you go to some brewpubs, by the time you finish reading the menu you are tired of hearing the word "beer"   and that is just the food menu. These menus are overthinking the beer and food thing. A lot of the pairings just don't work. You can marinate beef with beer. You can marinate pork with beer or braise or you can influence the sauce that goes with it…but you are not getting value added by just taking a certain beer and building a recipe with it. To see beer referenced ten or fifteen times on a menu…it's just too much…What we did here was try to pick some items that naturally go with beer. We also do some of the classics, like oysters with porter. We looked at it from the point of view of what we liked to eat with beer, not so much to do all the dishes with beer. It gets redundant at times to have beer mentioned four times within the beef section of the menu. We like to highlight a certain cut of beef such as a roasted tenderloin that goes beautifully with the India Pale Ale and really focus on that as being something we would recommend…You're not complementing it really. Wine dinners are a perfect example of what they do well. At a wine dinner you are never going to see pasta with tomato sauce on a tasting menu featuring French wines. You are going to see things that have taken thousands of years to develop as a pairing of flavors. For different reasons that farmer and his product went with that particular variatal grape—the one in the region. So that's really the path that we took. We wanted to have five or six well-placed beer referrals in the menu and no more.

The wait staff is well versed in the styles of the beers we brew here. They know what they all taste like and how they will go with anything on our menu.

Just as staff does with wines, they know more than enough to guide the customer to a good pairing. If someone is having a porter at the bar, and asks for a menu, the bartender knows that they can recommend the clams or oysters on the half-shell. There are some things that we do such as smoked salmon that go very nicely with Waterville Wheat, which has a nice spicy flavor that is a classic American wheat with a little fruit to it…Being a "publick" house we had to go with an Irish smoked salmon as opposed to a Nova Scotia.

We use fiber wheat as garnishes, and also as a table accent. This is related to a specialty beer we have at the moment, a raspberry wheat beer. Because raspberries are in season we took 175 pounds of black raspberry to make this particular brew. Phil Markowsky, our brewmaster, says that this beer can stand on its own as well as be an aperitif, and it goes wonderfully with chocolate, which we have been presenting as a dessert suggestion. But as a cooking ingredient…the color is so rich that it overtakes whatever you are working with.

Since the nights are getting cooler out here on the shore, I ran a boneless pan-seared pork tenderloin with porter-caramelized onions. It was just outrageous. The onions really picked up the coffee and chocolate accents of the porter, and there was no overkill. So I used the onions to smother the boneless pork tenderloin. It was terrific. That's a simple dish, but you have to go a long way to come up with anything as satisfying as that. We look for subtle infusions. I constantly tell our sous chef "not to make the beer the show. The food is the show and the beer is there to complement the food."

Environmental and social issues are part of the everyday world of the food service professional. As we have seen, a feel for local produce often leads to an awareness of local environmental issues. Taking that awareness a step further, Chef Cory Mattson feels that there are some moral and ethical issues involved in food preparation as well as the knowledgeable consumption of good beer and good food.

One of the most important balancing acts for Chef Cory Mattson is based on the cost efficiency of running a kitchen and the waste of food and creation of unnecessary garbage as a price for doing business. He feels that he has a social and, as he puts it, also a moral, responsibility to run an efficient kitchen and treat everyone in it with respect, and police his disposables, recycling when necessary and extended cooking, when possible. The basic idea for extended cooking is getting the most out of every part of every ingredient. Chef Mattson's illustration of using shrimp shells (usually thrown out in most homes and restaurants) as a base for a fine soup is a good example of thrift paired with a tasty method of getting the most from what would otherwise be untimely disposed of. This attention to environmental and social issues is part of the everyday world of the foodservice professional.

As we have seen, a feel for local produce often leads to an awareness of local environmental issues. Taking that awareness a step further, Chef Cory Mattson feels that there are some moral and ethical issues involved in food preparation as well as the knowledgeable consumption of good beer and good food.

CORY MATTSON
FEARRINGTON HOUSE, PITTSBORO, NC

I think a dark Lowenbrau was the second beer I had. I discovered that imported beers had more flavor than the major U.S. beers. That was in the 1970s and the import beers were just getting here and I was ready for them.

I'm not saying I was well versed about beer back then, but I immediately appreciated the flavors…They tasted so good. It was the same thrill as a kid biting into a fresh-from-the-tree ripe apple.

You can only get the true flavors from cooking with a moral and ethical approach to food. I mean, for example, everybody wanted to throw away shrimp shells, but I really appreciated using the whole shrimp. I do a lot of hunting and fishing and at that time I was doing a little trapping as well, so I very much enjoyed the idea of using everything from an animal. I still do…

This was reinforced later when I began studying the Cajun and Creole cooking that was happening in the early 1980s, and I was pleased to see that this had been going on all the time in Louisiana with the French influence on cooking using shells and fish carcasses and the like. It may not seem to be important to cooking with beer, but many of those chefs were using beer for their deglazing…. It was great because in rural cooking you use every part of an animal or food—you work too hard raising that crop or animal not to.

I didn't take beer in the kitchen much further than using it as a deglaze, or for batters— I use it as a liquid in batters all the time. In tempura batters I have always used beer. It doesn't matter if it is fresh or flat. Here in the restaurant I use fresh beer because it is available, but I do think it is traditionally a great way to use up flat beer because it adds a unique flavor. I used a lot on the vegetables as well as the fish and shrimp. I like the battered and fried cod. Real fish and chips is made with cod or haddock by a kid in England who really knows how to make it. You are talking about real soul food. Something that tastes good and makes you feel good is great. We are a fine-dining restaurant, probably the best in the state. For years all we had was Heineken and a lite beer like Amstel. What I have seen lately is a lot more different kinds of beer showing up in here. Obviously, we are more focused on wine, but I can see this thing coming…There are six or eight different beers now served here. Before dinners, and as an aperitif, they sell well. There are eight draft lines up there and that is six more than a year ago. Something is happening, especially if we are beginning to see this kind of an effect in a fine-dining restaurant.

Getting back to the moral part of food, beer, and enjoying both, I believe that an evening spent with friends and food and beer is a great way to spend an evening. I think I am seeing more of that appreciation for beer, rather than chugging it down to get smashed.

Beer with dinners in the home is one thing, but it is dangerous when young people celebrate outside the home with alcohol. It is a tragedy because beer is a wonderful beverage when part of the experience of enjoying a meal with friends. What we are seeing now is a lot of people who have grown out of the fast food phase, who still drink beer, but did get busy and take on the responsibilities of family and jobs. They are finding the brewpub-type places and that is encouraging. The brewpub concept is great in that it provides interesting food to go with good beer. It's not a case of just a place to go to drink as many beers as you can. These kinds of places take pride in their products.

For all the optimism about where the "beer explosion" is going, there are some who feel that the whole thing has gotten out of hand.

RICHARD WRIGLEY
PACIFIC NORTHWEST, SEATTLE, WA

The whole brewing thing is getting a bit weird…It's going overboard from my perspective. I'm leaving the United States. It has gotten to the point that it has nothing to do with beer any more and they have forgotten what beers are all about, that is, basically a drinkable social product to lubricate peoples' character. It is going off the deep end, so I am going to Japan where they have very good food. It is a different product.

I just got back from a month in Europe, Switzerland, Germany, Czech Republic, Austria, and I am horrified by the beers back here…having spent a complete month drinking purely drinkable beer without any complexities or oddities attached—just good beer in the classic styles. I came back here and found my own beers virtually undrinkable.

It isn't just what the brewers are doing. It is the purpose. The purpose now is to shock, overwhelm, and utilize gimmicks. So it will be interesting to see what will happen, but obviously there is a beer mania going on in New York.

To keep things in perspective, there are chefs, restaurateurs, and brewers who think the excitement surrounding the effort to change a menu so that it reflects a "beer theme" can be overdone.

MICHAEL HANCOCK
DENISON'S BREWING COMPANY, TORONTO, ONTARIO, CANADA

You see I like drinking beers…many kinds of beers, for that matter. I like beers from all over the world. I think that the volume that has been written about matching beer and food takes things a little far. In any case…I certainly think (some writers) take things a bit too far when they started matching beer with cigars, and beer with classical music…and drinking it in the nude. I enjoy drinking beer, making beer, and drinking it with food too. But there are times when I would much rather drink a glass of wine with dinner.

BREWPUBS, "BEER DINNERS," AND…

In the introduction to this book I mentioned that there are now at least two small breweries in each of the 50 United States, and each of the provinces of Canada. Many of these are "brewpubs," small restaurants with simple fare where the beer brewed on the premise is served only there. In many cases, there is little time or desire on the owners' part to develop a complex food menu to accompany the brewpub operation. They have enough of a challenge making sure that the flavor profile of the brew does not change dramatically.

In addition, over 50 restaurant-breweries have been established in the United States. These are serious restaurants with a "house brewery" on the premises. Here, the owner usually has both a chef and brewmaster on the payroll. The brewmaster ensures the quality of the beer and the chef has the challenge of delivering a menu of dishes that will show both the culinary skill of the chef and the talent of the brewmaster. In these restaurant-breweries the food ranges from uncomplicated to the point of gaining the restaurant notoriety.

The successful brewpubs of just ten years ago were, for the most part, rather elemental in their menu. Nevertheless, the pride that the brewer took in the beer was usually reflected in the attention paid to the quality of each dish offered on that menu. The dishes were slight variations on basic grilled sandwiches and simple side dishes. With a few exceptions, the majority of the restaurant-breweries have followed the logic that their objective is to offer the freshest produce, meats, vegetables, and beer. Freshness is the essential ingredient to success on both sides of the establishment. Beer is always best fresh from the brewery, as fresh produce is the most important ingredient to well-prepared dishes.

Today there are also a number of fine-dining restaurants, some of which have contributed to this book, that have very professional chefs in charge of their kitchens. These are chefs who are interested in more than just beer. They are also offering dishes on their regular menu that include beer as an important flavor ingredient. These fine-dining restaurants, although not breweries, take just as much care with their beer as they do with their fine wines. Beer has certainly found a place on the tables of some of the finest restaurants in the United States and Canada. This is most evident with the attention paid to the growth of "beer dinners."

THE "BEER DINNER"

A beer dinner, sometimes called a brewmaster's dinner, follows very closely the rituals of a wine-tasting dinner. Each course, prepared with ingredients that may include beer, is paired to the specific beer served with the dish. In some cases the rather serious atmosphere of the wine-tasting dinner is also reflected in the atmosphere of the beer dinner, although the latter tends to be much more relaxed after the second course. No matter how serious the beer and food pairing, there is a certain Gemütlichkeit about the enjoyment of beer that transcends its overly serious appreciation.

Beer dinners are becoming a special part of the culinary landscape. They are special social occasions that offer an opportunity for brewers to have their beers and ales enjoyed with particular dishes prepared by a chef working with the unique flavor of each brew. This synthesis of good beer, good food, and good friends is an experience that enhances all three of these "ingredients." Of course, economic reasons can also invite a knowledgeable restaurateur to explore the possibilities that beer dinners can provide.

WALT FORRESTER
PARKER HOUSE INN, QUECHEE, VT

I was looking for a hook to fill a slow night. We tried wine nights, but they were just a bust because there are too many people doing them. Then one of my beer salesmen brought along a rep from Kennebunk one day. He suggested that we might look into the idea of a beer dinner. He sent me a couple of menus of dinners that they had done. That planted the idea in my mind.

Cooperation between a beverage manager and a local beer distributor gives the chef a chance to discover new ways to expand a menu, or develop an incentive for regular customers to return for more than just the beer dinner.

CHEF WADE SIMPSON
LANTANA GRILLE, PHOENIX, AZ

We started in January of 1995 and, for our first few brewmaster dinners, we had a local distributor select beers. At first we had one dinner a month. Then, in August of 1995 we started doing them more often. Even from the first, we would have 30 names on a waiting list because I would accept only 60 persons for each dinner. I want the dinners to be fairly intimate. After every course I would come out and talk about the dish and the beer that was served with it. Then, in August of 1995 we started doing two nights in a row, about 120 covers all together. There are about 15 customers who make a point of coming to all the dinners. Some of them are home brewers, others come because we offer beers that they can't get to taste any other way. The rest are newcomers. About 50% are regulars. We have one customer who has been to all of our dinners. They have many of their family events here too. That is one example of people who come for the beer dinners and then come back at other times as well.

All of our menu items are paired. I don't do too many of my regular menu dishes with beer because if a line cook isn't paying attention, you run the risk of having to sacrifice an item on an evening's menu if there is a problem with the preparation. A lot of the "beer dishes" I save for the beer dinners.

The wine dinners are slowly losing their popularity, and I think a lot of the reason has to do with the pretentiousness of the wine dinner. The beer dinners are much more casual and people from all walks of life come to our brewmaster dinners. It is also turning some wine-dinner people around to the fact that some of the beers are just as, if not more, complex as some fine wines. You often get a varietal wine that is just not that dramatically different from any of the other varietal wines in the same category. On the other hand, you can have the hefe-weizen style of beer and there are many, many different hefe-weizens with completely different flavor profiles.

The wine people are especially turned on by the almost champagne characteristics of the Belgian lambics.

Belgian beer seems to have developed quite a following. Many beer dinners feature Belgian styles, sometimes a particular style exclusively. It might have been a Belgian beer that caused such a stir in Pennsylvania a year or two ago. That was a beer dinner that caught the attention of beer lovers and the state police. This is the way the story goes, according to Alan Schmidt, owner of the Farmhouse Restaurant in Emmaus, Pennsylvania.

ALAN SCHMIDT

FARMHOUSE RESTAURANT, EMMAUS, PA

The first beer dinner was more a pairing exercise. However, we were adventurous from the start. We started cooking mussels in Geueze and many of the classic combinations…carbonnades and that sort of thing. It worked out well because we had John on one hand, and he became a friend. There was the restaurant whether we were being adventurous. Then we had Shangy's (a local store) who was aggressive on their end of getting the beers for our market. We had a nice little triangle going here. The first one was overwhelming successful. It wasn't well advertised. We planned to do it on a Saturday night to see how it would do. We sold out in two days so we added a Friday night and that went just as quickly. The demand was still overwhelming so we did another Friday and Saturday night and those sold out immediately. At that point we realized that we were on to something. We could have probably booked another four nights with no problem, but we didn't have the facilities. We were doing them here in the restaurant in two rooms. One of the rooms held 30 people and the other held 20 .…John would rush back and forth from the two rooms as we staggered courses and give the same speech to each room…that was how we did the first one. From then we decided to use the barn next to the restaurant and do the dinners over there where we could do 80 people in one room all at once…and we started doing them there. Those were very successful and we were selling five nights of the "Christmas Beer" dinner and getting 80 people at each dinner. That was when the infamous "Beer Raid" occurred.

It was three years ago this December 11th, we had a Christmas Beer Dinner and held it in the barn. We had brought in Stella Nacht to the dinner because we thought it was one of the best Christmas beers we had tasted.

Since Stella Nacht is distributed in 20-bottle cases, and because the laws in Pennsylvania do not recognize a 20-bottle box as a "case," this beer cannot be sold in Pennsylvania. We had to purchase the beer out of state and bring it in ourselves. Our lawyer told us that since we were "giving" the beer to those who came to the dinner, and charging them only for the food and service, we were doing nothing different than offering guests a present. We never bothered to pay special attention to the fellow in a crew cut, dark blue windbreaker, and plain-toed black shoes who bought only one ticket, with cash, and insisted on a receipt. Of course he was a cop.

The local authorities didn't think much of our giving away beer. When the first beer was poured our mystery guest got on his cellular phone and, as a result, we got raided by the Liquor Control Board. They showed up with three state trooper cars, a van filled with state troopers…there were probably 15 agents here that surrounded the barn and went over all our inventory and confiscated most of it and….It was really obnoxious. The long and short of it was that we eventually won the case. We were in the right and they were in the wrong. They claimed that the reason that they raided us was not because we had the beer from out of state but that we were serving beer in an unlicensed premises. I got a fine personally for $200 for bringing the beer in from out of state because they didn't collect about $5 tax on that beer. The unlicensed premises was the barn next door to the farmhouse. The farmhouse is bisected by a town line. The bulk of the building is in abeyance but a portion of the building is in Upper Millford. When we applied for an extension to cover the barn, there was already a prece-dent in that a country club that had their license extended for the same reason. About a month prior to our application they were given an extension for their "half way" house on the golf course….When we applied for our extension we expected it to go through with no problem and the beer dinner was scheduled and all the rest. We were turned down and we were appalled. When we asked them why, they told us that since we were in another township in effect, they would be granting us two licenses because in this area there are grandfather clauses in all the licenses. So we appealed it but in the meantime our liquor lawyer told us that in order to get through the legal loophole all we had to do was give the beer away at the dinner. As long as we were giving the beer away, it wasn't a violation. It is no different from me offering you a beer when you come and visit me in my house. That was what, in effect, we did. The only caveat was that if someone came in and didn't want to pay for the dinner they would still have to be served the beer we were "giving away." That was fine with us. The State Liquor Board didn't take that approach. What they did was send an agent in undercover…. He was at the dinner and part way through he got up and called in the rest of his friends…. We should have known because he bought the ticket the day before, just one ticket and paid cash…so they came in and the confiscated all the beer and all the customers were booing and hissing. When I saw what was happening, I got on the phone and called the *Morning Call*, our local paper, and had someone here in 15 minutes. We were in the headlines in the morning edition!

There were eight letters to the editor and the paper did two editorials…only one letter was negative. Then we got press in almost all the beer publications to the point that when I go to a beer gathering outside of this area there are always conversations and it will come up, "Aren't you one of the guys that got raided?" So it did get us national press.

Mention in local press was icing on the cake for the Farmhouse. They were already back in the kitchen keeping things in perspective.

I don't think we have a signature dish that uses beer as an ingredient. What we have been pleased with in recent times is our *Hoegaarden sorbet*…it really brings out the characteristics of the beer, actually, I think the first time we made that was with a Blanch de Bruges on draft…. The spicy flavors in that beer can be very subtle when you are drinking it…you tend to not pay too much attention…when you add some sugar to the beer to make the sorbet, you really enhance those flavors.

We do enjoy the beer dinners. They are good for our bottom line. We have about one a month…We have done beer dinners with individual themes. We do the Pennsylvania Brewers dinner every year, and we have an organic beer dinner coming up. We also have an "eclectic" beer dinner coming up where we try to include the most unusual beers we can find. And then we have done seasonal beer dinners. We do Christmas beer dinner, and this year we are doing a New England beer dinner. To do an organic beer dinner a few years ago was almost impossible. Now, there is the Humes Brewing Company (Glen Ellen, CA)…I think all of their beers are organically produced. I'm not convinced yet but that would be great. Still, you have Pincus Müller from Germany, Jade from France, even here you have Perry's Majestic.

Next year we are toying with the idea of doing a canine themed dinner…using "Dog" beers. There are probably a dozen "Dog" beers in the marketplace, starting with all the Black Dog beers, to Old Growler, Red Dog…it goes on and on and on…"

LUCIE P. COSTA, CHEF-OWNER

NORTH PLANK ROAD TAVERN, NEWBURGH, NY

I grew up in Montreal, Canada where beer is not just a beverage - it is part of our heritage. The oldest brewery in North America (Molson's) was founded in Montreal in 1758. Besides Molson and Labatt, Quebec is home to an ever growing number of Micro Breweries.

When I opened my restaurant in the beautiful Hudson Valley upstate New York, both my husband and I had accquired a knowledge about beers through our many travels, especially in Europe visiting breweries in England, Belgium, and Germany. We wanted to have a beer list as exciting as our wine list. We were amont the first to offer an International Beer List which was featured in Nation's Restaurant News in an article by Mort Hochstein in 1984. We introduced beers like Sam Smith's Oatmeal Stout, Belgian Lambics, Trappist ales, and Smoked Bavarian beer. Back them it was pretty adventurious. People liked it and often made a detour on their journey just to have a taste of these special brews.

I like peasant food, earthy food. Root vegetables braised in beer, or roast venuson, pork and game, in general, are conducive to a good marriage of taste. Fall harvest in my favorite season to cook with beer. I like pumpkin soup with nut brown ale, salad dressinig with a wheat beer ot heather ale from scotland. The dressing becomes emulsified when you add beer to it and has a velvety creamy texture. Veal Rouladen with smoked Bavarian beer is ideal for a fall dinner. Homemade cheese croutons sprayed with beer and oven dried with a salad are best. Also, I like to brine duck breast and shrimp in beer and cold smoke it.

I dabbled with beer in the early 1980's. I used to do a pork roast with nut Brown Ale. Customers were interested in beer more as a beverage than as a style of cooking. In the last five years as people have become more educated about beers they relish Beer and Food pairing to the point that my Beer Dinners have become more popular than the wine tasting dinners.

Beers with a high hop content tend to become overly bitter when reduced too far. To be safe, most hoppy beers should not be reduced more than half when used as a base for sauces. If you need a reduction to concentrate flavors choose a malty beer such as an Octoberfest or a Brown Ale.

Chef Costa returns to her rural roots and offers us a special venison dinner that incorporates some very interesting sweet and savory flavor contrasts. **Roasted Venison Tenderloin in a Chery–Herb Crust, Glazed with Sam Adams Cherry Wheat Beer; Wilted Arugula Salad and Sautéed Mixed Mushrooms;** and **Herb Texmati Rice,** are a hearth warming example of a sweet and roasted flavors.

CHAPTER 3

The Beer Menus

The growth of beer dinners has challenged chefs and cooks at all levels of the restaurant industry. The following menus are examples of beer dinners hosted by the chefs who you have read about in the first section of this book. The menus follow the seasons of the year, from spring to winter, and the accent on regional and seasonal produce is obvious.

I have compiled this selection of beer dinner menus to illustrate the extent that chefs and cooks are taking beer seriously. You will note that there are some very complex menus offered. There are also a few limited menus that present familiar dishes with less familiar beers. With each menu is an explanation of what makes each pairing work, or not work. I have also tried to develop the theme of each dinner and track the direction that the chef was going in when the beer pairings were made.

In some cases the chef was allowed a free hand in determining the menu and the beers to present with each dish. In other instances the dinner was hosted by a particular brewery. In this case the chef is limited to the products of that brewery. This makes things interesting in that both the recipe and the beer are presented to special scrutiny.

Whichever situation determines the menu, there are a number of ways to pair beer and food. A contrast theme presents flavors that would ordinarily clash, but in this situation, achieve a balance. Each flavor is very evident but neither overpowers the other. A good example of this pairing is stout and chocolate. These two distinct flavors maintain their distinct flavors, but the combined flavors are fascinating rather than frustrating.

The alternative, complementary flavors, are more often used in a situation where neither flavor clamors for attention and the sensation is more of one flavor than a combination of two flavors. This is often the case when a beer is used in a vinaigrette or as part of a braised dish.

Here now are the menus.

THE OLD BAY RESTAURANT - NEW BRUNSWICK, NJ

Winter's End Beer Dinner

TUESDAY, JANUARY 30TH, 1996

SPECIAL GUEST: MATTHIAS NEIDHART

Assorted Fruits and Cheeses
paired with
Spaten Premium Lager

Soup of Escarole, Beans, Pancetta, and Plum Tomatoes
paired with
St. Georgenbraeu Keller Bier

Sweet Corn and Roasted Yellow Pepper Crabcakes
on Vegetable Straw with a Sherry Aventinus Beurre Blanc
paired with
Aventinus Wheat Doppelbock

INTERMEZZO

Koestritzer Schwarzbier & Berliner Weisse
with Woodruff and Raspberry syrups

Lamb Shank Braised with Ryebier, Shallots, and Potatoes
paired with
Schierlinger Roggen

Caramelized Breast of Pheasant served with Wild Mushroom Couscous
paired with
Sierra Nevada Celebration Ale (1995)

INTERMEZZO

Baltimore Holiday Doppelbock

Spiced Caramel, Apple, and Pear Napoleons
paired with
Anchor Our Special Ale '94 & '95

FINALE

Kulmbacher Reichelbraeu Eisbock

Coffee or tea

Menu prepared by A.J. Giordano, Ben Pollak, and Christopher Demetri

TASTING NOTES

A pilsner is a complement to most fruits and light cheeses. The light hop kiss of the pilsner and the dry finish contrast with the natural sweetness of the fruit and cut the butterfat content of the cheese, refreshing the palate.

A rich soup of beans and pancetta, with the sharp flavor of the tomato, and the bitter escarole, are all flavor foils for the rich keller bier. This beer is rich enough to sweeten the beans and enrich the pancetta. The slightly higher alcohol content meets the tomato acid head on and the escarole and hops dance well together.

The pairing of a doppelbock with a rather delicate crabcake is daring. The richness of the beurre blanc is matched by the warmth of the slightly higher alcohol content.

The Intermezzo here is a lot of fun. The addition of the woodruff (green) or raspberry (red) syrups to the goblet of very effervescent wheat beer is a sight to see. This traditional summer quaff for the citizens of Berlin is a nice reminder of the spring to come. This is one refreshing quaff

I think the selection of Sierra Nevada with the pheasant is the better of the two. The roasted pheasant and the roasted grains used in the ale are complementary. The earthy flavors of the mushrooms and the bold hops of the ale evoke images of rustic cabins and frosty nights.

A dopplebock is a rich, warm, introduction to a spicy, sweet dessert. The selection of the Anchor brews must have started conversations. There is always friendly competition between those who favor the Anchor product and the friends of Celebration Ale.

The choice of an eisbock as a "winter warmer" is a good choice, especially coming after the Anchor Our Special Ale. I will venture that it seems like a lot of dessert to me, but then I never turn down a Kulmbacher.

ALDEN COUNTRY INN - LYME, NH

◉ Beer Tasting Dinner ◉

MONDAY, FEBRUARY 19, 1996
SPECIAL GUEST: CATAMOUNT BREWING CO.

Grilled Shrimp over Rice with Ginger Sauce
paired with
Catamount Gold

Fresh New England Seafood Showder
paired with
Catamount Amber

Mixed Salad Greens with Shallot Vinaigrette Dressing
paired with
Sparkling water

Crispy Roasted Maple Duck with Cranberry Dressing
paired with
Catamount Pale Ale

Meringue, Fresh Shaved Chocolate Ice Cream, and Fudge Sauce
paired with
Catamount Porter

Menu prepared by Micky Dowd

TASTING NOTES

No risks taken here. The food was drawn from the regular menu at the tavern. The amount of beer served (one 12 oz. bottle per course per person) was excessive; one-half bottle with each course is plenty.

The layout, in three dining areas, gave no opportunity to speak with the guests as a group.

The appetizer was a nice pair: the ginger did not totally overwhelm, but complemented the Gold's crisp, Willamette hop finish. A bit more hoppiness could have been used. The Gold could also have been used in the sauce.

The chowder was light and refreshingly thin; Amber was an OK match; I don't think it could have stood up to a heavier, creamier chowder.

The salad was served without a beer. It would have been nice to try a beer based dressing with this one, substituting Catamount Pale Ale and malt vinegar for the acidity.

The entree was the most successful pairing of the evening. The dryness of the pale ale finish did well with the richness of the duck. The maple glaze and roasting paired well with the pale ale's roasted maltiness. Cranberries in the stuffing were faint, and did not overwhelm the beer or the duck. In retrospect, we could have risked even more of their tartness.

The porter stood up handily to the chocolate and fudge. Its dryness was an appropriate foil. We have yet to find a chocolate dessert that porter couldn't dance with.

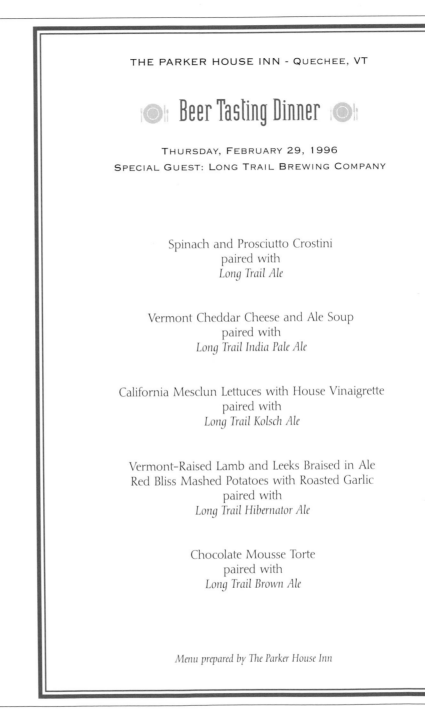

THE PARKER HOUSE INN · QUECHEE, VT

Beer Tasting Dinner

THURSDAY, FEBRUARY 29, 1996
SPECIAL GUEST: LONG TRAIL BREWING COMPANY

Spinach and Prosciutto Crostini
paired with
Long Trail Ale

Vermont Cheddar Cheese and Ale Soup
paired with
Long Trail India Pale Ale

California Mesclun Lettuces with House Vinaigrette
paired with
Long Trail Kolsch Ale

Vermont-Raised Lamb and Leeks Braised in Ale
Red Bliss Mashed Potatoes with Roasted Garlic
paired with
Long Trail Hibernator Ale

Chocolate Mousse Torte
paired with
Long Trail Brown Ale

Menu prepared by The Parker House Inn

TASTING NOTES

An ale is a nice pairing with this slightly rich mix of spinach and prosciutto, spread on a toasted piece of bread. The toast of the malt and the toast of the bread are complementary and just the background notes for the fun that the hops are having with the slightly bitter spinach and slightly salty prosciutto.

The pale ale is slightly bitter with a good measure of malt to keep the finish from getting too dry. This touch of hops adds harmony to the slightly sharp tang of Vermont cheese.

The salad course is presented with a Kolsch, a German version of a pale ale, but with a rich finish that contrasts well with the vinaigrette. The natural combination of green leaf and the hint of hops is most refreshing.

With any braised dish you will have a rich, meaty flavor, accented with root vegetables (a sweet note). The choice of a rich, strong ale is a good one. The rich flavor of the grain and the slightly sweet flavor of long braised beef, and the roast flavor of the potatoes, combine to satisfy even the heartiest appetites. A brisk hop finish refreshes the palette and extends the enjoyment of such a rich dish.

Chocolate is a tough match for any wine. Paired with a brown ale, a chocolate mousse takes on toasty hints. Served as a torte the brown ale helps cut the sweetness while enhancing the chocolate.

THE OLD BAY RESTAURANT - NEW BRUNSWICK, NJ

Winter's End Beer Dinner

TUESDAY, MARCH 7TH, 1996

SPECIAL GUEST: BEN MYERS

Assorted Fruits and Cheeses
paired with
Dry Blackthorn Cider

Crispy Oysters Served on Sauteed Spinach
with a Smoked Gouda Cheese Cream
paired with
Samuel Smith Pale Ale

Warm, Grilled Eggplant and Asparagus Salad
paired with
Saison Dupont

Ben's Special Duck Marinated in Bourbon and Brown Ale
paired with
Rogue Nut Brown Nectar

Osso Bucco of Veal with Wild Mushrooms
and Roasted Shallots, Served with a Ricotta Spaetzel
paired with
Sierra Nevada Celebration Ale (1995)

INTERMEZZO

Paulaner Salvator

Warm Chocolate and Dried Berry Chimichanga
with Vanilla Ice Cream and Sauce Anglaise
paired with
De Dolle Brouwers Stilla Nacht

FINALE

Chimay Grand Reserve

Coffee or tea

Menu prepared by A.J. Giordano and Chris Demetri

TASTING NOTES

Yes, there are times when a beverage other than a beer finds its way onto a beer dinner menu. In this case the cider is a refreshing effervescent complement to the fruit and cheeses. It also provides an interesting contrast to the pale ale served with the appetizer.

Let's see, we have briny oysters, bitter spinach, smoke and ale. These flavors are all in a position to complement each other in a special way. The deep-fried oyster has a nice texture contrast. When napped in smoky cream (a rich touch) and accented with the spinach (bitter to balance the brine), the refreshing mix of slightly sweet malt and a touch of hops ties the flavors together.

The grilled eggplant (smoky) and asparagus (that special grassy flavor unique to asparagus), when paired with the rustic Saison, evoke images of farmhouse and harvest time.

The bourbon and brown ale give this duck dish an almost caramel, and definite smoke, accent. The nut brown ale (a richer cousin to a brown ale) offers just enough hops to balance all the smoke, sweetness, and oils that duck is famous for.

Once again Sierra Nevada Celebration Ale meets up with a braised meat, redolent with shallots and escorted by rich cheese noodles. Any beverage served with this dish had better be able to hold its own. If not, the brew will seem to be thin and lifeless. The choice of a Sierra Nevada Celebration Ale puts all worry to rest. Here is an ale that has enough hops, malt, and alcohol to do the job and more. The hops cleanse the palate (a tough job here), the rich malt takes up with the sexy shallots, and the extra touch of alcohol seduces the rich noodles using its warmth to cut through the cloy that a cheese spaetzel can leave.

To insure that the dessert is properly announced, and the veal has a proper send-off, the Salvator is well chosen. This is a very "warm" beer (7.5% by volume) with almost plum overtones, and a touch of leather. A true after-dinner drink, or for sipping by a fire on a winter evening.

This is one magnificent desert. The Stille Nacht is a special beer, brewed only once a year. This adds romance to a decadent combination of liquid chocolate, and deep sweet berries awash in rich ice cream and sauce. The Stille Nacht enhances by allowing the taste buds to warm up and relax between the rush of riches here.

For those who have never had a well cared-for Chimay Grand Reserve there is only one recourse. Try it. This is not a high-alcohol after-dinner work horse. This is a sturdy, comfortable elixir that hints at pears and apples but delivers a dry grainy finish that is satisfying but not too filling.

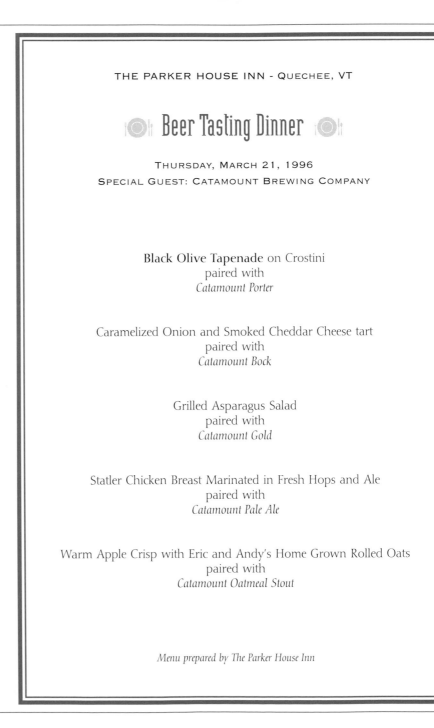

THE PARKER HOUSE INN - QUECHEE, VT

Beer Tasting Dinner

THURSDAY, MARCH 21, 1996
SPECIAL GUEST: CATAMOUNT BREWING COMPANY

Black Olive Tapenade on Crostini
paired with
Catamount Porter

Caramelized Onion and Smoked Cheddar Cheese tart
paired with
Catamount Bock

Grilled Asparagus Salad
paired with
Catamount Gold

Statler Chicken Breast Marinated in Fresh Hops and Ale
paired with
Catamount Pale Ale

Warm Apple Crisp with Eric and Andy's Home Grown Rolled Oats
paired with
Catamount Oatmeal Stout

Menu prepared by The Parker House Inn

TASTING NOTES

The cuisine we tasted rated the black diamond, like the more risky trails at the nearby Suicide Six and Mt. Ascutney ski areas. The Parker House is an easy drive from both and offers accommodations as well as fine dining.

Classics in a new context: the dinner menu took risks, but was firmly grounded in classic combinations. Eye-opening was the order of the beers. At a beer tasting, we taste beers in the context of other beers. Under those staged circumstances, we organize an orderly march from lightest to darkest, thin to heavy, light to strong, etc, one beer refers to another (in actuality or memory), precedent and subsequent. At a beer tasting dinner, on the other hand, the beers are recontextualized with accompanying dishes, foods, and courses. Any "natural"/intrinsic beer order goes out the window. We are tasting for different dimensions where the self-referential rules of beer tasting do not apply.

The tapenade and porter combination begged the question "Start a meal with a porter?" Why not? The saltiness of the olives and anchovies in the tapenade was reminiscent of the briney saltiness of oysters on the half shell…a classic combination with porter and stout. In this instance, the off-dry porter was an aperitif.

The pairing of the caramelized onion tart and Catamount Bock elicits this comment, "Spectacular combination, roasted, caramel, etc. The malty sweetness of the bock was a wonderful complement to the caramelized onions. I can imagine a white pizza bianco of caramelized onions, heavy cream, and prosciutto going well with the bock. Note that the relatively sweet bock was served after the dry porter. There is a progression at work here."

The grilled asparagus over white bean salad was simple and direct. "A classic. Where no wine dares to tread. The relatively faint acidity of the Catamount Gold worked well with the grilled asparagus."

The experiment of using real hops provided mixed results. "Astringently dry hopiness was unexpected in the succulent chicken. Less aromatic than I hoped, but the hop aromas are very volatile. The match was saved by the very sweet carrots and a wonderful sauce that included the pale ale."

Dessert also garnered mixed reviews, "No dissonance, no epiphany. The apple crisp and the oatmeal Stout were quite wonderful in their own ways, they just didn't connect, except by reference to the organic oats; a footnote, but not an illuminating exposition on either."

THE GRANITE BREWERY - TORONTO, ONTARIO

Brewers Banquet

SATURDAY, APRIL 20, 1996
SPECIAL GUEST: LOREN HART OF
HART BREWERIES, ONTARIO

Oxtail Soup
paired with
Hart Amber Ale (cask conditioned)

Chicken Kiev
paired with
Hart Valley Gold

Festive Ale Cake
paired with
Hart Festival Ale

Menu prepared by Clark Nickerson

TASTING NOTES

Here is an example of using dishes that are already on the menu and pairing them with the brews that show off the work of the brewmaster.

It should be noted that the Granite Brewery makes a policy of introducing Canadian beers, especially local beers, to customers. The restaurant has often hosted professional brewers organizations. The purpose of these dinners is to introduce a brewer and his beer, give the other brewers a chance to "grill" the brewer, and then enjoy a pleasant evening of "shop talk."

There is not much to analyze here. The pairings are straight up, pale to dark, light-bodied to rich.

Of special interest here is the cask-conditioned Hart Amber Ale. Served this way, the ale is only lightly carbonated but still tingles on the tongue and refreshes the palate in a way that more-carbonated beers can not.

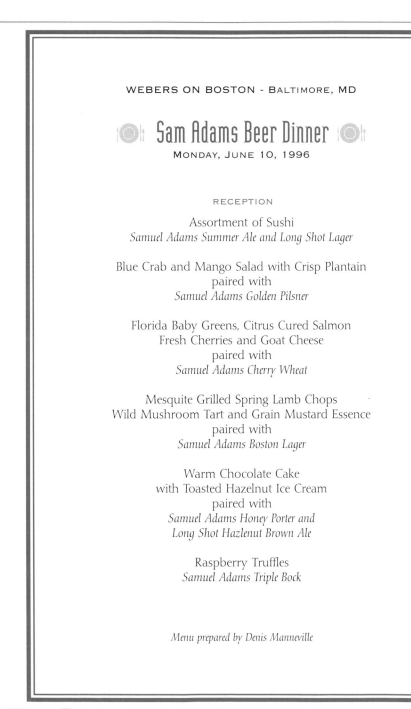

WEBERS ON BOSTON - BALTIMORE, MD

Sam Adams Beer Dinner

MONDAY, JUNE 10, 1996

RECEPTION

Assortment of Sushi
Samuel Adams Summer Ale and Long Shot Lager

Blue Crab and Mango Salad with Crisp Plantain
paired with
Samuel Adams Golden Pilsner

Florida Baby Greens, Citrus Cured Salmon
Fresh Cherries and Goat Cheese
paired with
Samuel Adams Cherry Wheat

Mesquite Grilled Spring Lamb Chops
Wild Mushroom Tart and Grain Mustard Essence
paired with
Samuel Adams Boston Lager

Warm Chocolate Cake
with Toasted Hazelnut Ice Cream
paired with
Samuel Adams Honey Porter and
Long Shot Hazlenut Brown Ale

Raspberry Truffles
Samuel Adams Triple Bock

Menu prepared by Denis Manneville

TASTING NOTES

One of the few sushi offerings found in this selection of menus. The interesting concept here is to let the beers take the spotlight. The selection of sushi allows guests to choose an item that fits their taste interest and try it with both beers.

The salad of crab and mango is a sweet combination of soft and firm textures. The crisp plantain chips contrast the two textures of the mango and crab. The beer served with this combination should allow the flavors of the salad dominate but offer the diner a refreshment, and the palate a chance to anticipate the next bite. The pilsner is a good choice because this particular pilsner is not only slightly richer than traditional pilsner, it is slightly more hopped.

The salad has cherries in it, and as an accent in the beer. The salmon and cheese offer a combination of silky, briny, and rich salmon and slightly tart/citric flavors from the cheese. The tart cherry flavors from the fruit and the beer contrast with the salmon and cheese but find a complement in the greens.

The grilled lamb brings a char and sweet flavor, with a firm texture, to the dish. The earthy flavor of the mushrooms and rich egg custard tweaked with the mustard bring a richness that has undertones of smoke, from the mushrooms. The beer chosen for this pairing is not as assertive as it could be. The reason for that is that the food is once again the star, the beer is accent rather than dominant flavor.

Again, the beer served (porter and hazelnut) gives the diner a choice between a dry and sweet beverage. The drier porter contrasts with the chocolate and ice cream. The complementary hazelnut flavors, once in the desert and once in the beer, is a bit much for anyone who doesn't possess a insatiable sweet tooth.

The chance to sip a Sam Adams Triple Bock is not to be passed up. The truffles are there to make sure your taste buds don't get too tipsy.

THE OLD BAY RESTAURANT - NEW BRUNSWICK, NJ

Summer Beer Dinner

TUESDAY, JUNE 25TH, 1996

SPECIAL GUEST: GEORGE RIVERS

FOUNDER AND PUBLISHER OF BARLYCORN

Assorted Fruits and Cheeses
paired with
Tabernash Heffe-Weizen

Chilled Sweet Carolina Bay Scallops, Calamari, Grilled Shrimp and Rock
Shrimp Marinated in Hoegaarden and Citrus Juices with Shallots and Basil
paired with
Hoegaarden White Ale

Cherry Wood Smoked Tenderloin of Beef
Served Sliced with Fried Green Tomatoes and an Onion Caper Relish
paired with
St. Georgen Kellerbier

INTERMEZZO

Schultheiss Berliner Weisse

Farm-Raised Rabbit, Braised in Alt Bier, with Wild Mushrooms
and Pearl Onions Served with Couscous and Honey Glazed Carrots
paired with
Im Fuchschen Dusseldorfer Altbier

Cherrywood Smoked Pork Ribs, Basted with Rye Beer
Served with Sauteed Fresh Corn and Beer Battered Vidalia Onion Rings
paired with
Schierlinger Roggen

INTERMEZZO

Aventinus Weizenbock

Rodenbach Red Marinated Fresh Cherries
in a Bread Pudding Served with a Cherry Sauce
paired with
Rodenbach Red

FINALE

La Chouffe Bok

Coffee or Tea

Menu prepared by A.J. Giordano, Larry Joffe and Chris Demetri

TASTING NOTES

Hefe-weizen is a summer brew. There are few beverages that quench thirst, dance on the tongue, and refresh the body like this beer. When paired with fruits and cheeses it reminds you of champagne. Then again, who needs champagne when a frothy wheat beer is close at hand?

The use of a citric flavor like wheat beer to marinate shrimp, scallops, and calamari adds not only flavor, but helps add a depth to the flavor of the particular fish. Paired with the beer used in the preparation adds context to both the beer and the food. Both pick up flavors and share flavors. The combination gives the diner a chance to follow the flavor. That can lead to finding some sweet touches where briny would be expected, especially with this dish.

The smoked flavor of the beef, tart green tomatoes, and sharp onion relish are all counterpoints to the rich kellerbier. Here is where you need a rich, malty beer to harmonize the flavors rather than point each one out to the exclusion of another.

Ask anyone who has spent summer in Berlin and they will have a story about drinking Berliner Weisse. There are few beverages more refreshing, especially with a splash of the traditional woodruff or raspberry syrup.

A full-bodied altbier (aged and higher in alcohol), keeps the rich rabbit dish from becoming too much. The trick here is to find a beer that is not too high in alcohol. An altbier, in this case, is a much better choice than a bock or double bock.

The pork ribs also need a beer to lift the richness to a level of satisfaction rather than a presenting a lethargic selection of dense flavors with little contrast. The roggen is a good choice because it is not going to compete with the rich flavors. Rather it combines the sweet onions and corn and allows the spiciness of the rye to come through.

The weizenbock is a more alcoholic wheat beer that the Hefe Weizen. This is a beer to use as the diners gather their thoughts and relax into the comfort of a desert.

In this case the sharp cherry flavor of the fruit and sauce is mirrored by the Rodenbach. The interesting thing here is that the beer is slightly sour. The accent is an interesting counterpoint to the tartness of the cherries.

THE OLD BAY RESTAURANT - NEW BRUNSWICK, NJ

Summer Beer Dinner

TUESDAY, AUGUST 2ND, 1996
SPECIAL GUEST: JAY MISSION

Assorted Fruits and Cheeses
paired with
Anchor Wheat

Prince Edward Island Mussels and Littleneck Clams
Simmered in Jersey Plum Tomatoes, Lemon Grass, Leeks,
and Stoudt's European Pilsner
paired with
Stoudt's European Pilsner Lager

Grilled Vidalia Onions, Crisp Arugula, and Spinach
Tossed in a Lemon Weizen Dressing
paired with
Tücher Heffe-Weizen

Lemon Pepper Marinated Halibut
with Fresh Corn, Roasted Poblano Pepper, and Cucumber Relish
paired with
Celis White

INTERMEZZO

De Dolle Brouwers, Oerbier

Sliced, Smoked Brisket of Beef with Wild Mushroom Sauce,
Whipped Yukon Gold Potatoes, and French Beans
paired with
Rogue Dry Hopped Red

Frozen Peach Lambic Souffle with Sliced, Fresh Peaches
paired with
Lindeman's Peche Lambic

FINALE

Rogue Old Crustacean

Coffee or Tea

Menu prepared by A.J. Giordano and Chris Demetri. Dessert by Steve Duggan of Pancho's.
Special thanks to Mountain Valley Brewpub.

TASTING NOTES

The light, very subtle, and very effervescent Anchor Wheat beer has a particular tang that is due to the flavor of the wheat. This tang contrasts with the sweet in the fruit and echoes the lactic tang in many cheeses.

Pairing a pilsner with mussels and clams combines two refreshing flavors, the salinity of the bivalves and the whisper of the hop in the dry pilsner. Here, the summer flavors of tomato (slightly acidic), lemon grass (for a fresh aroma), and leeks for a balance to the tomato, all add to a light but satisfying combination of sweet, salt, and bitter.

The salad course also pairs the beer used in the dressing with the beer served as beverage. Lemon and hefe-weizen are traditional refreshing icons of summer. The grilled onion, caramel hiding just under the char is a sweet answer to the slight bitter arugula and spinach combination.

Another wheat beer and fish combination. Here the Celis White echoes the flavors in the fish and the crisp flavor of the cucumber. The poblano chili keeps the taste buds from thinking they can take an early summer nap.

The pairing of the rich Rogue Dry Hopped Red with the smoked beef was a natural. The roasted malt echoes the smoked beef and the rather emphatic dry hopping challenges the sweet meat and adds an herbal flavor to the potatoes and beans.

Again, the combination of a beer used in a dish with the beer served as a beverage. There is no doubt that peach is a sweet, refreshing treat that mean summertime to many gourmands.

Wrapping up the meal with a taste of Rogue Old Crustacean is smoother than many spirits and just as easy to relax with. A fine postparandial libation.

THE OLD BAY RESTAURANT - NEW BRUNSWICK, NJ

Cask-Conditioned Beer Dinner

WEDNESDAY OCTOBER 18TH 1995
SPECIAL GUESTS: GARRETT OLIVER & SIR ANTHONY FULLER

Assorted Appetizers, Fruits and Cheeses
paired with
Oliver's Wharf Rat's Best Bitter

Roasted Duck with Wild Mushroom Strudel
paired with
Thomas Hardy Country Bitter

Gold Potato and Ale Soup in a Warm Bread Bowl
with Crumbled Cheddar Cheese
paired with
Brooklyn East India Pale Ale

INTERMEZZO

Left Hand Sawtooth Ale

Pan Fried Trout with Smoked Bacon Cracklings
Topped with Caramelized Onions and Lentils
paired with
Sierra Nevada Pale Ale

Sliced Yankee Pot Roast Braised in Fuller's E.S.B. with Roasted Potato Medley
paired with
Cask-Conditioned Fuller's E.S.B.

Brooklyn Chocolate Imperial Stout Mousse,
in Chocolate Cup with Crisp Wafer Cookies
paired with
Brooklyn Chocolate Imperial Stout

FINALE

Rogue Old Crustacean

Coffee or Tea

TASTING NOTES

Here the beer is the star. Cask–conditioned beer is especially enjoyable because it is so lightly carbonated and is served at cellar temperature, allowing all of the flavors to assert themselves and then assimilate into a balance of flavors that is unique to a well-brewed, well-cared-for cask-conditioned beer. This beer is a pleasure to pair with almost any food that needs a undercurrent of richness to enhance its own flavor. It is always interesting to see what chefs make of this specially conditioned brew.

In this case, the fruit and cheese is paired with a bitter style beer. Contrary to popular opinion, a proper British "bitter" is actually a slightly carbonated, slightly sweet slightly alcoholic brew. Its main purpose in this world is to serve as a "session" beer. This is a brew that is low enough in both carbonation and alcohol to allow the imbiber to survive a round in a British pub. It is a British pub tradition that when a group gathers each member stands all the others to a "round" of beers. It is considered poor form to duck out before you have stood your round.

The roast duck with wild mushroom strudel, when paired with the Thomas Hardy Country Bitter, recalls traditional British country fare. Both the richness of the duck and the full body of the beer support each other and accent the sweet rich flavor of the duck.

The soup in a bread bowl is a lot of fun at dinner. The pairing of the potato/cheese soup with the East India Pale Ale lets the very dry finish of the well-hopped beer revive taste buds that have been swaddled in the very rich cheese/potato combination.

The intermezzo of a rounded rich ale prepares the diner for a smoky, sweet fish dish.

A simple pan fried trout is enriched with the bacon cracklings and onions. The big bodied, very hoppy Sierra Nevada Pale Ale had more than enough muscle to foil the richness and accent the sweet flesh of the trout.

Now comes the culinary "pun." The Yankee Pot Roast was paired with the star of the evening–a British traditional cask-conditioned ale. And what an ale! The Fullers E.S.B. used in the braising and the E.S.B. that fills the pint glass both deliver the flavors (slightly spicy in the sauce because of the unique hops used in the brewing process are even more evident in a braising liquid than in the glass, where it is refreshingly bitter) that diners look forward to in a traditional dish and a traditional quaff.

The desert was especially created to show off the Brooklyn Chocolate Imperial Stout. (The recipe is featured in the recipe section of this book).

Once again the Rogue Old Crustacean brings a beer dinner to an end.

Fall Holiday Beer Dinner

TUESDAY, NOVEMBER 14TH, 1996

SPECIAL GUESTS: DAVID EDELSTEIN & PIERRE CELIS

Assorted Fruits and Cheeses
paired with
Stoudt's European Pilsner

Celis White Marinated Bay Scallops,
Nestled in Field Greens and Pears, Tossed in Celis White
paired with
Celis White

Sweet Potato Soup with Roasted Pecans
paired with
Anchor Our Special Ale '94

INTERMETZO

Stoudt's Honey Double Bock

Veal Medallions in a Wild Mushroom Sauce served with
Whipped Yukon Gold Potatoes and Asparagus Spears
paired with
Celis Grand Cru

Roasted Muscovy Duck with a Sundried Cherry Sauce
with Spaghetti Squash Tart
paired with
De Dolle Brouwers Stilla Nacht

INTERMEZZO

Rogue Mogul Madness

Brooklyn Chocolate Mousse Torte with a Chocolate Stout Sauce
paired with
Brooklyn Chocolate Imperial Stout

FINALE

Brauerei Huerlimann Samichlaus

Coffee or Tea

Menu prepared by A.J. Giordano and Chris Demetri. Dessert by Steve Duggan of Pancho's.

TASTING NOTES

The pairing of Stoudt's European Pilsner with the fruit and cheese plate offers the full-bodied brew a chance to develop the flavors of the fruits and cheeses. Fruits that are not local often do not get a chance to fully ripen before being picked. They are often gassed to "ripen" them. What they lack in flavor is replaced by the combination of their less than sweet flavor with the slightly more than dry flavor of this pilsner style beer.

Scallops once again find their short rest in the arms of Celis White will spice them up for an appearance with slightly bitter greens and the cool, sweet pear. There is a tank to wheat beers that pair very well with the saline flavor of scallops, oysters, or heaven forbid, caviar.

The nutty combination of sweet potato soup and roasted pecans both highlight the roasted malts used in the Anchor Our Special Ale. The well-hopped brew stands up well to the thick soup.

While taste buds anticipate a rich meat entree, they are treated to an aperitif style beer, the rich, almost candy-flavored Stoudt's Honey Double Bock. Mouth feel is a real treat here. This is a well-attenuated beer that feels lighter than it is.

A real winter warmer, veal medallions with a sauce rich in rustic aroma and woody flavors, is escorted by comforting potatoes and that very adult vegetable, asparagus. The Celis Grand Cru is a very nonthreatening choice here. The wheat tang is less evident than the Celis White but the fuller body lends an accent to the slightly sweet flavor of the veal. I would suggest a beer with a higher hop content.

Roasted duck, with a powerful cherry sauce needs a strong beer with medium body but a major alcoholic punch to keep the very rich duck and cherry flavors from overwhelming a palate that has just been relaxed by the veal and Grand Cru combination.

The second intermezzo presents a rather heavy beer as a prelude to the massive Brooklyn Chocolate Imperial Stout.

The chocolate mousse and Imperial stout call to mind the appetites of Catherine the Great of Russia. But that's another menu…

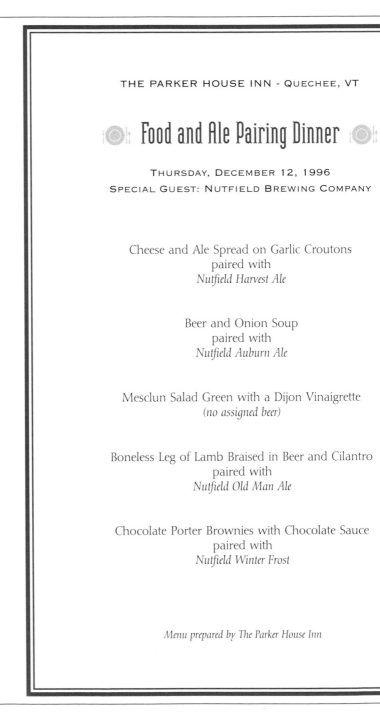

THE PARKER HOUSE INN - QUECHEE, VT

Food and Ale Pairing Dinner

THURSDAY, DECEMBER 12, 1996
SPECIAL GUEST: NUTFIELD BREWING COMPANY

Cheese and Ale Spread on Garlic Croutons
paired with
Nutfield Harvest Ale

Beer and Onion Soup
paired with
Nutfield Auburn Ale

Mesclun Salad Green with a Dijon Vinaigrette
(no assigned beer)

Boneless Leg of Lamb Braised in Beer and Cilantro
paired with
Nutfield Old Man Ale

Chocolate Porter Brownies with Chocolate Sauce
paired with
Nutfield Winter Frost

Menu prepared by The Parker House Inn

TASTING NOTES

This dinner presents the beers of the Nutfield Brewing Company in Derry, New Hampshire. The dishes were all dishes on the menu of the Parker House.

The cheese and ale spread is certainly a flavorful foil to the Nutfield Harvest Ale. The garlic of the croutons takes on a sweet, almost nutty flavor when paired with a toasty ale.

The tradition of beer/onion soup paired with the beer used to make the broth is a tried and true combination. The grain flavors are both lighter and lower in cholesterol than beef broth.

A salad dressed in a simple vinaigrette could use a festive brew full of carbonation (to take the edge off the vinegar), slightly sweet (to contrast with the bitter greens) and pleasant to look at (bubbles and smiles are great dinner conversation starters). I surmise that there was no beer in the Nutfield portfolio to take on the challenge.

A boneless leg of lamb is a fine companion to a strong ale such as Nutfield Old Man Ale. The unique flavor of the cilantro lends almost a hop-style finish to the pairing.

Once again beer shows how well it pairs with chocolate. Once a show stopper, this combination needs to take on a new dimension (a bourbon sauce perhaps?).

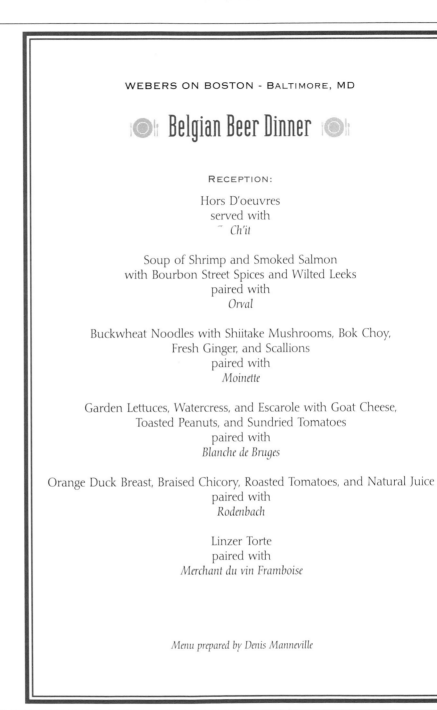

WEBERS ON BOSTON - BALTIMORE, MD

Belgian Beer Dinner

RECEPTION:

Hors D'oeuvres
served with
Ch'it

Soup of Shrimp and Smoked Salmon
with Bourbon Street Spices and Wilted Leeks
paired with
Orval

Buckwheat Noodles with Shiitake Mushrooms, Bok Choy,
Fresh Ginger, and Scallions
paired with
Moinette

Garden Lettuces, Watercress, and Escarole with Goat Cheese,
Toasted Peanuts, and Sundried Tomatoes
paired with
Blanche de Bruges

Orange Duck Breast, Braised Chicory, Roasted Tomatoes, and Natural Juice
paired with
Rodenbach

Linzer Torte
paired with
Merchant du vin Framboise

Menu prepared by Denis Manneville

TASTING NOTES

Now we see how a chef, well versed in the beers of Belgium, handles a "Belgian Beer Dinner."

The chef starts right off with a beer from France? Yes, Ch'it is brewed by Brasserie Castelain, Wingles, France. This is a very fruity beer, with pear and apple aromas. The rustic flavor goes very well with any hors d'oeuvres.

There is a taste of New Orleans, shrimp, and salmon, in the soup. The pairing with the Abbey beer Orval, is a fine choice. The salty flavors of the salmon and shrimp pair with the fruity flavor of the Orval to open slightly different flavors to accent the basic sweet and salty.

The next stop is Asia, with ginger and scallions taking to the Moinette bottle-conditioned Belgian ale with the same enthusiasm that Belgians took to Indonesian-based dishes brought home by the veterans of the Belgian Asian outposts.

From the California school of salad making we are presented with greens, goat cheese, and sun-dried tomatoes. The tangy flavor of the opaque Blanche de Bruges pairs very well with the lactic tang of the cheese and the acid tang of the tomatoes.

Orange and sour cherry flavors meet with the pairing of the duck and the Rodenbach. The roasted chicory and roasted tomatoes fill the slight bitter contrast to the sour-cherry flavor of the beer and the rich orange flavors of the duck.

The always festive Framboise is a happy suitor for the aloft, but buxom, linzer torte. The statement and echo of raspberry, first in the torte and then in the beer is playful and refreshing, rather than dense.

CHAPTER 4
Raw Bar and Appetizers

Here is where pale pilsners waltz smartly with shellfish, salmon (dressed or undressed), and trout, smoked of course. Soft pale ales, sipped while enjoying slices of sausage and almost any cheese, also whet the appetite for a fine meal.

As sure as the tide, raw shellfish, particularly oysters and clams, have survived falling in and out of favor. I believe that they, like a good beer, are an acquired taste and appreciated only after many are sampled. In New York City, Chef Rick Moonen can be appreciated by any friend of beer. His menu, especially his appetizers, are all very beer-friendly. As he tells it, beer and oysters are underappreciated. It took a side by side tasting to make the point. As he tells the story, it was a tasting of East Coast oysters.

RICK MOONEN

OCEANA, NEW YORK, NY

One of the most interesting events I have attended was an oyster tasting. There were over a dozen East Coast oysters on the half-shell. It was very interesting to taste the same oyster from two or three beds in three different areas. You could tell by the flavor where the oyster had been harvested. What was even more interesting was the flavors that you found when you paired those same oysters with different beverages. We had the choice of champagne, dry sherry, or Guinness stout. Each beverage brought out different flavors from oysters that had been harvested from the same bed. I thought that the slight salty flavor of Guinness went especially well with many of the oysters from various harvest areas. That was a real education.

APPETIZERS

Appetizers, those special treats from the kitchen served just before a dinner, are where the diner gets the first impression of how the dinner is going to progress.

Unique pairings heighten expectations of additional surprises, white traditional pairings of sterling character announce a special attention to quality through understatement.

CHEF AND DIRECTOR OF OPERATIONS KEN WOODBURY
OZARK BREWING COMPANY, FAYETTEVILLE, AR

We have an appetizer of barbecue ribs because barbecue is, naturally, very big down here. In fact, about 80% of the restaurants down here are smoked or barbecue. An appetizer like this fits into a regional theme without making us a "barbecue place." It gives the people what they want. Even when we had the fine-dine upstairs we had the barbecue ribs on as an appetizer. They sold like crazy. They were originally just on the fine-dine menu upstairs. You have a hard time imagining these fine southern genteel ladies just picking up these ribs and gnawing on them. They loved them.

From oysters to barbecue, the appetizer is meant to tease the diner and suggest the skill with which the rest of the dinner will be handled. Close attention to freshness is absolute, and imagination should also be part of the recipe. Chef Michael Perselay used his beer as a complement to the rich flavors of a duck enchilada.

CHEF MICHAEL PERSELAY
TRIUMPH BREWING CO., PRINCETON, NJ

We started out with an appetizer of slow roasted duck with wild mushroom enchilada and goat cheese that had chipotle in it. We put a smoked porter with that to go with the smoked flavor in the chili peppers…It was slow roasted so they could work their flavors into the dish.…We were going to go with the stout with the oysters but we decided to do something a little bit different because we had slow roasted the duck so the smoky flavor in the porter seemed to go with that, and we looked for something a little briny tasting to go with the oysters, and the hops in the IPA seemed to fit.

BLACK OLIVE TAPENADE

Walt Forrester, owner of the Parker House Inn, in Quechee, VT, has done three beer dinners and each one had a unique appetizer. The most interesting has been a tapenade based on chopped black olives.

We were doing a beer dinner with the beers from Catamount Brewing Co. We wanted to start with a Catamount Porter and the usual pairing with a porter is oysters. The porter flavors, roasty malt and dry hops needed something briny.

Our **Black Olive Tapenade** was just what we were looking for. I don't really have a recipe for it. We use dry-cured, pitted black olives, some chopped garlic, a few capers, and a touch of hot pepper flakes and a splash of rum, for warmth. We put that altogether in a blender and chop it, careful not to purée it. Then we add just enough oil to get it the right consistency. Spread that on thin toast and serve it with a porter beer and the combination is very interesting. We also had a chicken breast marinated in ale with fresh hops…

But that is another chapter.

CHAPTER 5

Soups

One of the most comforting foods on any menu is a steaming bowl of soup or a hearty stew. From the simple broth all the way to a bouillabaisse, beer is right at home. Used at the beginning of such classics as French onion soup, or as the finishing touch to a smooth cheese soup, beer has an opportunity to share its rich malt body as well as offer a touch of bitter to balance a touch of sweet flavor in the likes of a chowder.

The first example of how beer can be used both in the initial preparation and in the final stage of a recipe is presented by Chef Cory Mattson.

SHRIMP SHELL SOUP

CORY MATTSON
FEARRINGTON HOUSE, PITTSBORO, NC

I got into using beer in the kitchen when I began to understand "deglazing," a better term to use than "reduction." I got into deglazing when I was getting seriously interested in cooking and was working in a serious restaurant called Landwares on the Delaware River in Lambertville, New Jersey.

It was there that I also started to work with shrimp shells. At that time the more enlightened restaurants were using things for the essential ingredients in their signature dishes that most people would throw away. One of the things that separated the fine restaurants from the others was their ability to use something like shrimp shells instead of throwing them away. We would peel and then bread shrimp for frying, or steaming, or grilling, and then cook the shells with some vegetables, garlic, and seasoning. Then we would deglaze the pan with beer to get an extended cooking process. The result was a rich sauce that could be used in a number of ways. You could just throw butter in and strain it for a smooth sauce for sautéed fish, or grilled fish steaks. Or you could add cream to it for a sauce. Add a gallon or two of stock and you had a nice soup. It was unique because it was a flavor that you can't buy.

What I would like to share with you is an oriental style **Shrimp Shell Soup** that is based on the shrimp shell deglazing procedure with some vegetable seasonings, dry seasoning, and, to give it an oriental flavor, ginger, scallions, and lemongrass. The deglaze with beer extends the cooking process because the shells release more color, more gelatin, aroma, and probably more nutrition too, the longer you can extend the cooking process. Then comes the interesting choice. You can rehydrate it with either stock, water, or beer and see what you end up with . Lightly garnished with a dumpling, a pot sticker, or even simple rice or thin noodles, and you have a very nice soup.

Chef Andy Finestone offers a cheese soup, but with a sweet twist. The stone beer he uses has a sweet finish that smoothes out the sharp lactic tang of a hearty cheddar cheese.

STONE BEER CHEESE SOUP

ANDY FINESTONE
BOSCOS, GERMANTOWN, TN

This has got to be one of the most interesting examples of combining a brewery and a restaurant into a place where beer, pasta, food, fun, and history are all part of the experience. Bosco's menu is basic Italian, the beer served is "Famous Flaming Stone Beer," and the restaurant can be found in Germantown, Tennessee.

Here is a truly unique brew. Technically called "steinbier," it takes its name from a unique way of brewing practiced in Germany when there was no iron to make brew kettles with. The tradition continued until the end of the nineteenth century. Basically, the brewer heated local stones in the fire until they were beyond hot. These stones were tossed into huge wood pots filled with the sweet wort. The heat from the stones not only brought the wort to a boil, it also caramelized some of the malt sugar in the wort and created a special smoky/sweet flavor in the beer.

As a homebrewer, Bosco's brewmaster Chuck Skypeck discovered the story of steinbier. When he took on the position at Bosco's he was determined to brew something unique to the restaurant. As luck would have it, Bosco's has a brick pizza oven, so the place to heat the stones was there. A few experiments determined the best local stone to use in the process.

Chef Finestone's **Stone Beer Cheese Soup** highlights the unique flavor of the steinbier brewed at Bosco's. To make an authentic recipe you will have to go to Germantown to get some of their special beer. If you don't have time to visit, I would suggest substituting a dark Bavarian bock or double bock. The key is to have a fairly sweet brew with a good measure of roasted malt used in the grist, lightly hopped, with a slightly smoky flavor. The alternative is to combine a Salvator with a few ounces of Rauchbier. Make sure to taste the combination to ensure that there is enough "smoke" in the mix. The smoke flavor is what makes these two recipes so interesting.

Chef Jack Sedivy of the Silo Microbrewery in Louisville, Kentucky claims that he got involved with beer in the kitchen quite by mistake. He just happened to buy a restaurant that had a brewery attached. Still, he will admit that a number of his dishes do go very well with a fresh brew.

WHITE BEAN AND TASSO SOUP
RED BEANS AND RICE WITH ANDOUILLE SAUSAGE

CHEF JACK SEDIVY
SILO MICROBREWERY, LOUISVILLE, KY

I don't mean to put you on a stump, but the cuisine of Louisiana didn't include beer. It is back-woods type food mixed with French and Caribbean influences. I try to avoid terms like Cajun because people think you add a lot of hot spices like cayenne and Tabasco. That goes for the "blackened" business too. What it does mean is a cuisine that is full-flavored and spicy…Beer goes well with spicy food…it is full-bodied and the food does not overpower it….Most of the stuff we have on the menu needs beer to balance the spiciness, rather than pairing with wine. I don't know how well beer goes with our shrimp salad or crawfish salad, but just about any crisp lager sure goes well with our **White Bean and Tasso Soup.** Another good pairing here would be the **Red Beans and Rice with Andouille Sausage** and the Derby City Dark. That is the real "down home" item on our menu.

An interesting variation on a dessert soup is suggested by Chef Wade Simpson.

CHEF WADE SIMPSON
LANTANA GRILLE, PHOENIX, AZ

I did do a raspberry lambic soup with chocolate mousse dumplings for dessert on an Octoberfest menu. I used the Lindemans Framboise in a raspberry soup instead of the champagne. I used the lambic beer in the chocolate mousse that was shaped into a dumpling and placed in the center of each bowl of soup.

Chef John Dickenson takes a rather powerful cheese and pairs it with a well-hopped, hearty ale.

GORGONZOLA ALE SOUP

CHEF JOHN DICKENSON
WYNKOOP BREWING, DENVER, CO

One of the fun things I have discovered is that you can add one of the cellar temperature beers to whatever you are cooking, such as a sauce or soup, and the flavors carry over just remarkably well. One of my favorite soups to use beer in is a **Gorgonzola Ale Soup** based on potatoes, onion, Gorgonzola cheese, our Railyard Ale, and a touch of cream.

SCOTT & JAMIE'S TEXAS LOVERS' CHILI

CHEF SCOTT COHEN

THE STANHOPE, NEW YORK, NY

At the seventh annual United States Beer & Food Tasting, hosted by the New York Chapter of the American Institute of Wine and Food, at Bridgewaters at the South Street Seaport complex in lower Manhattan, Chef Scott Cohen offered samples of his Chili-rubbed Tuna with Sesame Seaweed Salad and Cous Cous. Paired with a well-hopped brew, the warmth of the spice and the slightly salty flavor of the tuna were both complemented by the rather bitter beer. The secret to the successful pairing of such a highly hopped brew with such a spicy dish was the effect of the hop flavoring. First, the bitter and spicy flavors became more complex when combined. Just as important was the cleansing effect that the dry hop flavor had on the palate, renewing anticipation of the next round of flavors. Such a good pairing of food and beer flavors was impressive, showing not only a solid understanding of the basics of the flavors that make up a well balanced beer, but a particularly "beer-friendly" appreciation of the dish by using the spicy flavors to enhance the appreciation of what otherwise could have been perceived as a overly hopped beer. A few weeks later, I was looking forward to getting a chance to chat about this particular pairing with Chef Cohen in his office at the Stanhope Hotel.

It was surprising to hear his less than enthusiastic reaction to my thesis that there was a culinary revolution going on, with particular attention being paid to the flavor pairings of fine cuisine with the explosion of flavors offered by the growing number of "microbrew" beers. When I offered the theory that this offered a real opportunity to develop menu ideas and "tasting dinners" based on beer rather than a wine list, the conversation became "all-business," and the talk turned to the efficient and effective presentation of a menu in a fine dining establishment. Did beer fit into that picture? Chef Cohen assured me that the few major European and Canadian lagers and pale ales seemed to meet most demand at the Stanhope. His restaurant is, after all, known for a very good wine list.

He was, however, philosophical about the precedent set by the growth of boutique wineries of the 1980's.

Today beer is always a subject of conversation when people are talking about food. It's part of the interest in brewpubs and microbreweries. It is a lot like the California wineries in the 1970s and 1980s. Although many Americans are now experimenting with high-margin imported and domestic beers, the overall perception of a great food and beer pairing is still "steak and beer." Popular brand European and Canadian beers are the most called-for beers here. There are customers who will ask for a specialty beer, but that is the exception.

The use of beer in the kitchen at the Stanhope is somewhat limited by the fairly traditional menu of fine-dining dishes based on wine sauces or preparation. Chef Cohen would much rather drink a crisp, cool pilsner-style beer than cook with it.

The rich brown brews such as ales, porters, and stouts do add a special touch in some of the more rustic dishes such as in marinades, chili, and braised meats. Dark brews go very well with well-done meats such as Texas barbecue, especially with the tougher cuts of meat used in this style of cooking.

Beer adds dimension, the sweet flavor of malt can stabilize spicy flavors and cut sharp flavors. Perfect for dishes of well-done meats as a rule, rare meats need savory and well-done cuts of meat need a sweet finish, notes Cohen.

In the end Cohen decided to share his **Scott & Jamie's Texas Lovers' Chili** recipe not only because it goes nicely with beer (although there is no beer in the recipe), but as a "first date": the preparation and enjoyment of this particular recipe has been known to lead to a red-hot Texas romance. Just ask Chef Cohen, or his wife Jamie.

CHAPTER 6

Fish

When pairing fish and beer, the distinction between heavier, oilier fish, and flakier, sweeter fish makes beer selection fairly straightforward. As a rule, the sweeter, richer beers pair best with the stronger-flavored fish. Drier, more delicate beers pair best with the more delicate fish. Preparation is also a key to determining which beers pair with certain fish. Steaming or poaching calls for a delicate, dry beer such as pilsner or pale lager. Grilled or smoked fish take on the flavors of the fuel used to cook the fish and are best enjoyed with darker, richer brews. Then, there are the exceptions to the rules. The following chefs each offer unique observations on preparing and pairing a wide range of seafood with the fruits of the brewer's art.

CHEF STEVE FOOTE
BRISTOL BAR & GRILL, LEAWOOD, KS

Wall-eye, scrod, and trout have a delicate flavor that goes with a drier, hoppier beer. Tuna, swordfish, and salmon go best with the heartier beers such as stout. The delicate fish are usually best when sautéed or poached. If you are poaching or lightly sautéing a filet of fish in a breading, it would be a key to go to a drier, lighter-flavored beer. Those styles of beer can also be used in the cooking process. Steaming with those styles of beer, and using them in a sauté as opposed to wine, would be very interesting to try. Dry stout or stronger red ale would lend itself to marinades or reductions for sauces. Some chefs tell me that the residual sugars in the darker beers also have a tendency to caramelize on the outside of the fish and lend a nice color as well when used as a marinade, or basting sauce for grilled fish.

Sweet beer creates a conflict with grilled fish. The fish has a subtle flavor. A lot of the fish do. We have wall-eyes and some of our ground fish from New England such as the sole or scrod which we bake or sauté. These have very delicate flavors that need a drier beer to go with them. We suggest some of our drier wines as well to go with those fish in the same way. A pilsner-style beer would go very well with the more delicate-flavored fish and then the fuller beers such as the stouts or the ales will go more with the tuna, salmon or swordfish off the grill.

One of the things that I learned from the wine pairings was that the food enhances the flavor of the wine as much as the other way around. I have always thought that. I think that the food helps the flavor of the wine, and likewise with the beer. If you have a more hearty-flavored beer, the flavor is not going to get lost. We do some red sauces form the southwest with some of our fish, and you need a beverage that is going to hold up to it.

This unit of the Bristol Bar & Grill has just opened, but the first one has been a Kansas City landmark for 15 years. The interest in microbrews or craft beers has just begun to catch on in this area. In fact, I just was visiting Boulevard Brewing Company, a local brewing company here in town. They have just come out with a stout beer that I really enjoy. I have just introduced the staff to this "food-friendly beer," and suggested that they might tell our customers that it isn't as heavy as it might look. In fact, it has a smoky flavor and a slight bitterness, that lends itself to the grilled fish. It also has a nice texture and dryness to it, which is a contrast to the sweeter beers that don't really go well with a hearty grilled fish.

It has only been in the last year that our customers have started to look at beer more seriously. Beer has always been considered something that goes with a lunch; trying to move it onto the dinner table is a challenge right now. We are just introducing this dry stout as a dinner beer and suggesting some of the red ales to go with some of the grilled steaks and fish. In fact, I have some salmon and swordfish marinating in Boulevard's stout right now.

Since we are doing some mesquite cooking, I think there are several beers, especially this dry stout, that will work well with a grilled fish. I think that the slight bitterness and slight smoky flavor of the stout will make it compatible to mesquite grill. The hearty steaklike flavor of swordfish should work very well with it. I'm interested to see how the salmon marinates in it and cooks on the grill.

MUSSELS IN BELGIAN ALE

SAM BARBIERI

WATERFRONT ALE HOUSE, BROOKLYN, NY

Mussels, shellfish—fish in general—the brine flavor in them comes through with a light beer, for example halibut poached in beer. In the dish **Mussels in Belgian Ale**, the ale has candy and corkiness to blend with the brine flavor. Balancing the sea flavors is good with Belgian malt (almost candy-sweet) yeast (banana and cooked apple esters) and the process lends a winey acidity to combine the flavors. In Hoegarten-Celis, the touch of cardamom is especially interesting in pairing with seafood. Start with broth—use Hoegarten on draft—shrimp stock/clam broth to make a base. Then deglaze the pan, but don't make it the main ingredient—it's for background flavor to stand out at the end. Bring to just a boil, then simmer.

ALE-BATTERED SHRIMP AND ONION RINGS

CHEF BILL DOWNEY

EDWARD MORANS, NEW YORK, NY

One of the comments I have been hearing when the subject of deep-fry batters comes up is the fact that when you use beer in the batter, especially a rich malty brew, you get a nice malty aroma to the dish when presented at the table. You can smell the malt, which is something you lose if you don't use beer. The heat from being fried in hot oil drives off the aroma of the fried batter; with a rich beer the aroma is slightly sweet and nutty. There is also the slight caramelization of the sugars in the beer when they come in contact with the hot oil. Fish, onions, or other firm-fleshed vegetables, and shrimp have traditionally been battered. These ingredients all give off steam when cooked. This also blends with the aromas that come from the ingredients used in the batter. Wheat flour, rice flour, and beer all contribute unique properties to the flavor and aroma of the batter. The addition of the aromas created by the battered ingredient are another essential factor in the aroma. When the unique aroma of the battered ingredient blends with the bready aroma of the batter and the sweet aroma of the beer, the effect is much more enjoyable without the addition of the nutty-sweet aroma brought to the table by the addition of beer.

ALE-BATTERED COD WITH RED CHILI TARTAR SAUCE

DAVID MILLIGAN

BRICKTOWN BREWERY, OKLAHOMA CITY, OK

The best selling dish on our menu is an **Ale-Battered Cod with Red Chili Tartar Sauce**. We use our Copperhead Amber ale that gives it a nice toast color. Normally a beer batter is with a lighter beer but an amber beer gives it a nice color and you can really taste the rich malt flavor. Chef Milligan suggests that for the best results "Use the freshest fish you can get. If you can't get cod you can use halibut. Delicate portions of fish may fall apart with this preparation."

BAKED SALMON WITH HEFE-WEIZEN, SWEET CORN, AND FENNEL

JOHN DICKENSON
WYNKOOP BREWING, DENVER, CO

The spicy flavors of hefe-weizen and fresh fennel are contrasted by the richness of the salmon and butter and the sweetness of the corn.

Traditional sauces are made by reducing wines and other liquids, and I have found that when you do that you tend to accentuate the bitterness. Sometimes this is ok but most of the time it puts a flavor there that your palate just doesn't expect. Our brewer generally takes a free hand with the hops.

One of the things about cooking with beers is that there really are no rules; you use your palate and judgment, but we are at a frontier of experimentation with combining and pairing.

The cooks upstairs know I encourage them to experiment. Sometimes I veto them and sometimes I say yes, but it is all in fun.

SALMON TARTARE WRAPPED WITH SMOKED SALMON

CHEF RICK MOONEN
OCEANA, NEW YORK, NY

One of my favorite pairings is St. Christoffel, from the Netherlands, an all-malt, full-bodied, dry pilsner-style beer, with my **Salmon Tartare Wrapped with Smoked Salmon**. The malt stands up to the saline flavor of the fish, the acid of the vinaigrette dressing, and the richness of the egg and salmon. The dry hoppy finish cleanses the palate perfectly for the next taste of salmon.

FIERY SHRIMP

DAN RUSSO
VIRGIL'S REAL BBQ, NEW YORK, NY

Here at Virgil's we have many examples of regional barbecue, but I personally like what happens when I enjoy a cool pilsner and our **Fiery Shrimp**. Based on a compound butter of rosemary, cayenne, and red pepper, the shrimp are sautéed, doused with fresh shrimp stock that is reduced with some scallion. Fresh butter takes the edge off the super-hot spices. It makes a very nice presentation when it is served on an oval plate with a side of rice. It is tough to choose just one beer that would go with this dish. I think I would choose a Pilsner Urquell, or a Rolling Rock, or a Warsteiner, or Dock Street.

Moroccan Halibut with Pilsner Butter

Corporate Chef Michael Perselay
TRIUMPH BREWING CO. PRINCETON, NJ

The next menu will have some of the beer dinner items, such as **Moroccan Halibut with Pilsner Butter** added to our regular menu. What I am trying to do with the new menu is to change the focus...I think that beer goes with all kinds of food. You go out and have sushi and there is a beer for that. Why can't we do what everybody else isn't doing? And show them that it all works with beer. I would like to take a wine menu and show people that those same foods work very well with properly paired beers. That is what I am thinking when I sit down to write a menu. I am not limited because I work with beer.

Norwegian Salmon Fillet in Honey Porter

Denis Manneville
WEBERS, BALTIMORE, MD

My brother introduced me to Belgian beers about 12 or 14 years ago. That was when I began tasting some of the more unique beers that are typically Belgian. He was visiting the French part of Belgium quite often because his father-in-law lives there, and he was bringing back some very unusual beers—some of then very high alcohol content like the Chimay and Trappist beers. That is when I started understanding those beers.

Then, last year, we did a couple of beer dinners, and a representative from Sam Adams asked if we would be interested in doing a beer dinner using the Sam Adams line of beers in the recipes as sauces and dressings, that sort of thing. That was very successful. In the past we would simply pair the beers with the dishes on the menu. This was different in that we used the beers in the dishes as well. One of the more interesting dishes we tried was a **Norwegian Salmon Fillet in Honey Porter**. This was one of the first times I used a beer in a dish. I was very surprised to discover the effect that the flavors of the beer had on a dish that I was very familiar with. There were many new flavors here and the combination of the flavor of the salmon and the sweet and smokey flavor of the beer was very enjoyable.

Sushi and Pilsner?

Laura Simoes
THE INN AT MAPLEWOOD FARM, HILLSBOROUGH, NH

One of the things we talked about was substituting beer for the rice-vinegar. The rice vinegar, when you are making sushi, creates a moisture barrier between your hands and the sticky rice, and beer can do that, and also lend a bit of flavor to the rice. The beer would be a sweet, dry flavor rather than the sharp flavor of the vinegar. And, of course, the rice vinegar is what you would typically use to make sushi, but I would rather use the beer, especially if I am serving beer as a beverage to go with the sushi.

I find that a beer like Catamount Amber is especially good with sushi. I like the fact that it is dry and, with an amber like Catamount Amber, there is a fruitiness about it. And there is the acidic and sweet combination with sushi. Especially when you get a taste of the wasabi on the back of your tongue. The beer mellows that flavor out. In the past I found nothing went better with sushi than saki, so it was a pleasant surprise to find that Catamount Amber Ale went so well. It was something that I hit on by mistake.

Cooking with beer is such a new thing. There are so few experts—I am sure that a lot of the chefs you are talking to will tell you that there is a lot of trial and error going on. So it is nice when you hit on something that works the first time and you don't have to play with it too much.

You would start out with some maki, which is the seaweed that you use to wrap the sushi. And on that you would brush, instead of the rice vinegar, some fruity amber beer…also make sure to moisten you hands with the same beer.

Making the **Sushi Rice** is a little bit more work than most people realize. You have to steam the rice and than let it sit with a towel over it to absorb more of the moisture, and give you a very sticky style of rice. It has to be sticky to hold its shape for the sushi and the other ingredients as well.

You brush the Nori with the beer, using a pastry brush, and then you take a little bit of beer on your hands and shape the rice in kind of a line. Then you make an indentation along the line of rice with a chopstick and fill that with wasabi, that wonderful, bright green, I guess they call it a "horseradish" but it tastes like nothing we have in this country…and then on top of that you layer whatever you are going to be using in your Maki roll. I will be honest with you and tell you that I am not a big fan of raw fish.

If I am serving a sushi as an appetizer, or as an entrée, I use cucumber and make a Kappa Maki or Oshinko, which is a pickled radish that I can get at a specialty store in Sommerville, MA. …Other options are to make a California Roll with avocado and processed crabmeat. The processed crabmeat holds together better than fresh crabmeat…and then there is a Boston Roll, which is crab meat and cucumber—that is a little bit different from a California roll. Then I would layer that on, not too much, and then start at the end that has the rice on it and roll it up. It is that easy. The beer adds a little bit of moistness to the Nori, which makes it adhere better to the rice. It also keeps the rice from sticking to your hands when you are shaping the sushi…Once you roll it up you can slice it into one-inch lengths and it comes out looking like those beautiful round pieces of sushi you get at Japanese restaurants.

THE INN AT MAPLEWOOD FARM

One of my favorite kinds of sushi is Dbi sushi, which is a shrimp sushi, a shrimp that has been deveined and butterflied and placed on a ball of rice, with a little bit of wasabi on top and another shrimp on top of that. I think that if you marinated the shrimp in beer and steamed it in beer, almost poach it, very lightly so that it is just pink and white—you don't want it to get tough—that would also go well with an amber ale.

I think that cooking with beer is like cooking with wine in that I like to drink the same beer that I have been cooking with. That is why I especially like the **Summer Porter Chowder (with Butter Crust Bread)**. It only calls for a half bottle of Porter beer, so I can sip the rest of the beer while I am cooking! Not on the job of course, but when I am home and cooking in the kitchen with friends it is great.

The rice recipe I am sending you calls for a vinegar mixture and I wouldn't substitute beer for all of that. Also, I don't know how "serious" cooks feel about this, but I use a rice maker. It make a lot of rice quickly and easily. If you buy the short-grain Asian rice, it comes out perfectly sticky and you don't have to fool around with the recipe I am sending you. Although this recipe works, I think you could do it in a rice cooker. You can buy it in any store that sells kitchen appliances. It is electric and I believe ours might be a Hamilton Beach brand, but Japanese companies have been making them for some time and now American companies are making them as well. They are used all over Europe. My husband's family lives in Portugal and they have been using one for years and years. We are finally catching up with them in this case. It is very convenient, for one thing, and for brown rice, which takes a lot of time and stirring to cook properly, the rice maker makes it very simple to just plug in and leave it to cook itself.

SABA SUSHI (MACKEREL SUSHI)

Sushi is one of the most popular Japanese foods. There are several kinds, including "nigiri sushi," an oval rice ball covered with a slice of raw fish or shellfish; "chirashi sushi," seasoned rice covered with raw fish slices and fried egg cut into strings served in a box or a bowl; and "maki sushi," a long rice roll wrapped in dried seaweed (nori). Another type of sushi, called "saba sushi," is especially popular in Kyoto.

To make saba sushi, one side of the salted and vinegared mackerel is placed on cooked rice, then covered with a strip of seaweed (konbu) and wrapped in a decorative bamboo sheath. The scent of the bamboo moderates the natural fish aroma, and gives this type of sushi its distinctive flavor.

Why is saba sushi so popular in Kyoto, which is surrounded by mountains? In the old days, mackerel preserved in salt were carried on horseback and on foot all the way from Wakasa Bay in the Sea of Japan. During the journey, the salt flavored the fish to create the right taste. Kyoto people love saba sushi so much that the route from Wakasa to Kyoto is still named "Sabakaido" (The Mackerel Route).

CHAPTER 7

Fowl

Our friends in the world of wine have spent many a festive evening enjoying "coq au vin," roast chicken in white wine, and chicken breast with wild mushrooms in a champagne sauce. Not to be outdone, the Belgians are quite proud of the traditional favorite breast of duck with fresh cherries and Kriek beer. A true "comfort food," chicken, in its many recipes, brings a flavor combination of the juicy, sweet, mild flavor to the table. Chicken takes on truly comfortable dimensions when combined with the earthy pungency of wild mushrooms, or a rustic melange of root vegetables and fresh garden herbs.

In his **Big River Rocket Red Chicken**, Richard Hamilton, corporate chef at Big River Grille & Brewing Works, Chattanooga, TN, recognizes the importance of "comfort food" to his customers. "Flavors are very much comfort feelings for people," says Hamilton. "It is important to carry those feelings over into the food."

At City Tavern, a casual restaurant in California, Chef Eric Hofflinger starts out his essential chicken stock with a touch of beer to add to the rich flavors,

Here I'm using a mixture of Newcastle Brown Ale and Redhook Ale. I just quickly deglaze and add my chicken and beef stocks. These stocks add a nice depth to all the dishes they are used in, especially my onion soup. Now that's real comfort food. With the addition of chicken stock it is less heavy, but just as flavorful.

John Maxwell at Allen's in Toronto, Ontario, gives the nod to ethnic "comfort food" such as chicken. Although Allen's is a traditional Anglo/Irish restaurant, Maxwell includes some dishes that are not traditional Irish/British dishes. "For example, we have chicken quesadilla with spicy black bean salsa," says Maxwell.

Also in the regional/local theme is a chicken dish from the kitchen of John Gilliam at the Ozark Brewing Company in Fayetteville, AR. Here, deep in "Tyson Country," chicken takes on even more importance on the menu.

We do a **Braised Chicken in Hefe-Weizen Ale** that is marinated in a weizen dressing. We take a half chicken and season the cavity after it has been marinated for about 24 hours in a weizen vinaigrette dressing. It picks up the flavors of the weizen, and then we slowly braise it in the oven and serve it over sautéed vegetables. It is almost in the old country style French bistro food, hearty food that utilizes chicken, which is very big down here. I wouldn't say it is a signature dish, but it is very popular.

SZECHUAN CHICKEN

CHEF OTTO RICE
R. P. McMURPHY'S, VANCOUVER, WA

One of my favorite things to cook, and I do it all the time, is Szechuan chicken with spicy green beans and a Bachelor Bitter to go with it. My friends just go nuts every time I do it. In fact we're doing it tomorrow night for a big party. This dish demands a Bachelor Bitter…it has a nice hoppy finish with a light body—not real dark, filtered, from Deschute's Brewery in Bend, Oregon. I don't necessarily pick out a beer, but that one has always worked out. Tim sent me home with a gallon of beer that just happened to be Bachelor Bitter and that's what we did that night and we have been doing that combo ever since. I imagine that the hoppier finish leaves a nice flavor in the mouth that cleanses the palate from the spicy chicken…I still don't know why they call it a bitter because it never seems bitter to me. It seems to take the heat off your tongue.

CHICKEN BREAST MARINATED IN BOSTON ALE

DENIS MANNEVILLE
WEBERS, BALTIMORE, MD

The menu is casual bistro food. American/French…The bistro foods pair well with the hearty beers because of the hearty spiced flavors of the food.

I am planning to eventually move some of the dishes from my beer tasting dinners to the regular menu. We are just on the edge now. When we do specials they are often some of the dishes we use for the beer dinners. We have a core menu and then we have three or four specials a night. So yes, especially with the beers we feel we can add some of those dishes to the menu. We will use these dishes to promote some of the fall and winter beers. We are not looking at the German seasonal beers; we are looking at the local beers.

As far as using beer in the dishes, I think that the dinner with Sam Adams was very interesting. We worked up recipes such as **Grilled Breast of Chicken Marinated in Boston Ale** to pair with the beers that the folks from Sam Adams suggested we might use as a framework for our menu.

BEER MUSTARD MARINADE

MARK LEWANDOWSKI
TIED HOUSE CAFE AND BREWERY, MOUNTAIN VIEW, CA

The other thing we do here is make all of our own sausages for all three restaurants. We make theme here at the Alameda location and deliver them fresh to the other three restaurants…right now we are making, basically, all chicken sausages. The best-selling dish we do is the chicken sausage in dark beer with roasted garlic…and we use our stout or Ironwood Dark in it. We offer them as both an appetizers and entrée. We make five or six different chicken sausages and have at least two varieties on the menu at once. When we first started making them we were making (for all three restaurants) about 200 pounds a week, now we are making over 450 pounds a week

For my winter menu I am working on a wort and molasses mahogany roast chicken, and so I have taken the wort from the Oktoberfest, punched it up with molasses and some soy for a salty flavor, and marinated half chickens in that. Roasted, with the relatively high sugar content in the marinade, it should come out with a nice mahogany color. Right now we have a **Beer Mustard Chicken Marinade** that can be used to base any number of recipes. It's a good marinade because it incorporates the sharp mustard with the dry flavor of the hops and the effects of the mildly alcoholic beer on the chicken.

BREAST OF DUCK

CHEF DANIELE JOHNSON
BISTROT BELGIQUE GOURMANDE, OCCOQUAN, VA

Bistrot Belgique Gourmande

I began to seriously use beer in my kitchen as soon as the number of Belgian beers available in Virginia grew to more then nine, which was all we had when we opened the restaurant! My favorite beer and food pairing? You can't do any better than the traditional **Breast of Duck with Fresh Cherries and Kriek Beer**. That is real comforting food.

CHAPTER 8

Meat

Now we get to the "meat" of the menu. Ales and rich bock beers are especially suited for service alongside grilled and roasted meats. The roasted characteristics of the darker grains pair quite well with the slightly smoky flavor of grilled meat and with the subtle rich sweetness of roasted and braised birds. In this chapter we will discover the secret to selecting the best lamb, and the key to perfectly grilling a beef steak.

LEARNING ABOUT LAMB

Keens Chophouse is one of the oldest restaurants in New York City. It is best known for a dish of mutton chops. A conversation with Chef Robert Johnston reveals the basics to preparing lamb as well as the key to understanding how to decide which beer will go best with the lamb dish you have on your menu.

Lamb is a fairly strong-flavored meat. The older it is when butchered, the stronger the flavor. The most important thing to remember when shopping for lamb is that there are essentially two types of lamb sold on the market. The first is U.S. Western lamb, the other is New Zealand spring lamb. The main difference between the two is that the Western lamb has a tendency to be a little older than New Zealand and has more flavor. The New Zealand lamb is usually shipped almost frozen. This can cause it to be a bit "mushy" because the freezing breaks down the musscle tissue as the liquid in the cells breaks down the cell walls. I prefer to buy Western lamb. It is usually a larger piece of meat and is less likely to be shipped in shrink-wrap. The larger cut of meat is easier to handle and the shrink-wrap can change the flavor of the meat. The two best cuts to purchase from a grocery store are the "rack" chops or the "loin" chops. Of course, for the adventurous, there is the "butterfly" leg of lamb. This is good for stuffing and serving at large dinners.

I do not suggest using marinades. This involves too many flavors and detracts from the natural flavor of the meat. The best way to prepare lamb is to simply rub it with salt, pepper, garlic, and herbs (rosemary or tarragon). Get your broiler as hot as you can get it and grill the chops until well marked. Try to make sure that the chop is no thicker that 1.5 inches. Any thicker and the meat will char on the outside and be much too rare in the middle. Grill on each side for about 3 to 6 minutes. The object is to use the high heat to "caramelize" the outside. The next step is most important. The lamb should be "finished" (allowed to finish cooking to the desired doneness—in a oven set at about 400°F). If you are cooking on an outdoor grill, remove about half the coals and cover the grill. Let the lamb "finish" for about 6 to 8 minutes. In a 400°F kitchen oven, you should cook for about 8 minutes. These cooking times will result in a medium-rare chop."

LAMB SHANK IN PALE ALE

RON KEEFE

GRANITE BREWERY, TORONTO, ONTARIO, CANADA

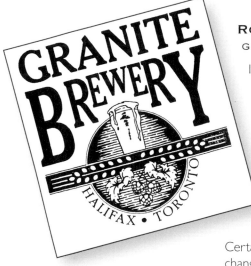

I wouldn't say that we have a particular focus. It is very general. We have six pastas on the menu. We have a number of entrées, from beef strip loin steaks to orange Szechuan chicken, lamb curry…we have a number of curry dishes on the menu because in Toronto there is a huge Sri Lankan presence, and many of the immigrants have gravitated into the food service business and become cooks and kitchen staff. Some of them have really evolved over the last few years into very interesting cooks and chefs. So, of course, we have a lamb curry on the menu. It goes very well with not only the darker ales, but the lighter ales as well.

The chef plays with some of the beers, and you must have a very educated palate to pick out what beers he uses in many of our dishes. Certain dishes call for a lighter beer or a strong beer, and this results in some changes in flavor and color. We did some really nice sauces with the beer. A **Braised Lamb Shank in Pale Ale** was one of the highlights of one of the dinners.

OSSO BUCCO

ANDY FINESTONE

BOSCOS, GERMANTOWN, TN

We make our pizza dough out of beer. And sometimes we will do beermaster dinners—some dishes cooked with beer and some paired with beer. We use our own beers and the brewmaster will talk about his beers. We have done about five or six. The last one we did, last month, turned out very well, so we will start doing one every couple of months. It has gotten to the point that people who hear about our beer want to come to the dinners and learn more about the beer and how to serve good beer with good food. Most of our customers know good beers and want to know more about them. This is what makes the dinners so successful. We have had around 30 people, we could have had more but I do not want it to get out of hand.

We had a four-course meal, including steamed cockles in a cream ale, then a fruit salad with tropical fruit dressing served with a wheat beer, and then some **Osso Bucco á la Boscos**. We also served a Porter pie—a "death by chocolate" style cake made with porter.

With Mediterranean cooking you have to go with the lighter flavored beers or possibly an amber. When you cook these beers down, the bitter flavors are less noticeable. After browning the osso bucco I deglazed the pan, then I added a mirepoix and orange juice concentrate. The citrus seems to blend the flavors a little bit. Then I added the Stone Beer.

GUINNESS-SAUCED LAMB SAUSAGE

JOHN ZENGER
RIVER PLACE HOTEL, PORTLAND, OR

I have used Guinness recently in a dish I call **Guinness-Sauced Lamb Sausage on Tomato Fettuccine.** Interestingly enough it makes a real nice pasta sauce. I have used particularly the stout; Porter works, but not as well. The goat cheese cream and beer may sound a little unusual, but if you actually do it you will be amazed. We were doing a lamb sausage with a lot of shallot garlic and mushrooms and sort of deglazing with the Guinness Stout, finishing it with cream and working the goat cheese in, melting it into the sauce as a thickening agent. The pasta was a fettuccine at the time, which was a nice combination.

BEEF STEAKS AND GRILLING

CHEF GEORGE MOLINARI
FRANK'S RESTAURANT, NEW YORK, NY

Frank's is a family-run restaurant in the Chelsea neighborhood on the west side of Manhattan. Not far from the meat-packing district, and close to where the Hudson River piers once welcomed merchant marine shipping from all over the world, this was a blue-collar restaurant that showed its Italian heritage with pride.

The Molinari family has had a Frank's in the neighborhood for two generations. The "old Frank's," as I have been told, needed more space and a real facelift. Today it sits on a corner of a block that gets its teeth rattled by the stream of trucks that growl in and out of loading docks and warehouses. I will not venture into the connection between honest manual labor and the appreciation of simple honest food. This is not to say that quality isn't appreciated. Frank's has both honest value and quality. Even more to the point, Frank's serves this French country beer that goes so well with a seared rare rib of beef that even wine mavens have been known to order a bottle. (Ask for a bottle of St. Amand and you will know how a fine steak and a fine beer complement each other in a most remarkable way.)

Although Frank's now sits on a corner, and has a special room, behind glass, for cigar smokers, it has not lost the comfortable feel of a family restaurant. On a weekday evening the clientele are a mix of well-dressed businessmen enjoying steak and beer before continuing their evening attending a sports event at Madison Square Garden, and local couples and extended families enjoying the good food and conversation.

Of particular interest are the well-aged beef steaks that are served here. All steaks are aged 4 weeks and are either rubbed with hearty Cajun spices or grilled au naturel. Chef Frank suggests that these hefty portions of beef are nicely matched by a particularly well chosen French-Flanders "French Country Ale" called St. Amand. Brewed by the Brasserie Castelain, in Wingles, France, this beer is especially suited to grilled meats. Chef George tells the story:

About ten years ago one of my wine salesmen came in and, after taking my usual order, showed me a bottle of French beer. He told me that he thought it might make a good addition to the selection of tap beers we carried. I really liked the look of the bottle. It was one of the first cork-finished 22-ounce bottles of beer I had ever seen. The flavor was certainly richer than the beers I had on draft. When I had it with a steak I was even more impressed. The slightly sweet flavor of the malty beer went very well with the slightly smoky flavor of the grilled meat. The dry hoppy flavor at the finish was a perfect palate cleanser for the richness of the well-aged steak. I was so impressed with the beer I decided to add it to my inventory. As far as I know, at the time, we were the only place in town to carry St. Amand. Today we sell about two cases a week of this beer.

Chef George is, of course, very particular about choosing his steaks. Beef should always be purchased from a butcher who ages his meat. This gives the flavor of the meat a chance to develop and become much more tender than if it is simply cut from a side of beef or sold soon after being shipped to the butcher in a vacuum-packed plastic package. The best method of aging beef is to cool-air dry age it. This involves hanging the side of beef in a cool, dark, relatively dry cold box (refrigeration unit).

When preparing a well-aged steak, it is important to keep things as simple as possible.

HOW TO COOK BEEF STEAK

The ideal method of preparing beef steak is to grill it on an open flame grill at temperatures over 1,000°F. Since few home ovens can reach this temperature, a gas flame broiler, set at as high a temperature as possible, is best for home preparations.

Steaks should be salted and peppered before grilling/broiling. Contrary to popular belief, salt will not draw any juice from the meat when the steak is quickly seared on both sides.

Thin cuts can be quickly sautéed in a salted, almost white-hot cast-iron skillet. In this case you salt the pan, not the steak. This provides just enough seasoning and also a crust to aid in containing the juices. The reason the skillet should be almost white hot is to instantly sear the surface of the steak. When quickly seared on both sides, the juices are sealed in and the meat will not get dry and tough.

Steak should be served accompanied by a starch and fresh vegetables. Potatoes are ideal because they provide a balance to the rich beef flavors. Many steak houses (Frank's included) often offer either spinach or another bitter green as an accompaniment to grilled beef. The bitter greens contrast well with the smoky sweetness of the beef

SHORT RIBS WITH CHIPOTLE PEPPERS AND WHEAT BEER

MARK LEWANDOWSKI

TIED HOUSE CAFE AND BREWERY, MOUNTAIN VIEW, CA

The item that I have served at some of the beermaster dinners in the past has been the **Braised Short Ribs of Beef with Chipotle Peppers and Wheat Beer**. You can either go with a wheat beer to cleanse the palate and give you a burst of flavor with each sip, or a dark beer that would intensify the rich reduced flavors of the peppers. It really depends on the temperature of the day. If it is cold and raining outside you want a dark beer. If it is hot I will pair a lighter beer with it to take the edge off the rich roast flavor of the beef and peppers.

I have found that in cooking with beer you really can not add enough beer into it to really have that flavor really come out. With beer you have to coax the flavors of the beer out. The beer that you are serving with the entree…some of the ingredients that are supporting that flavor…it is more of a combining ingredient…more in the background. Not like a wine reduction that can be the tip of the flavor profile that you are looking for. It is kind of a different feel to it."

PORK

CHEF JOSEPH ELORRIAGA

MIRICLE GRILL, NEW YORK, NY

The beer style I would like to focus on here is the Vienna, which is all but extinct outside of Mexico. The style is characterized by an amber to reddish-brown lager of medium body. There is a noticeably toasty quality to the emphasized malty flavor, with enough of a noble hop bitterness to give the beer a balanced, dry finish. The resulting product is a quaffable beer, yet interesting enough to linger on while you are reaching for the next one. The most important quality of a Vienna-style beer here is that it starts out with a malty sweetness and finishes dry, making a perfect accompaniment to spicy foods. The sweet malt soothes and blankets the burning palate and the dry finish washes it all down, leaving the diner ready for the next fiery mouthful.

Heat is a very important element in cooking because it is neither a flavor nor an aroma, it is a sensation which adds a whole new dimension to a dining experience. The dish **Grilled Pork Chops with a Yucatan Orange-Chili Recado** is indeed spicy and is much influenced by the cuisine of Mexico, and more specifically, the Yucatan.

There is an obvious German-Mexican fusion to this recipe as well as the beer style. Bavarians and Austrians like to drink a malty beer with their pork because the sweetness in the malt matches the sweetness in the pork meat. The bitter finish and the crisp acidity of the beer helps cut the fat in the pork as well.

There is also a reccurring theme of toast in this combination of food and drink. The Vienna and Munich malts used in Vienna-style beers are roasted lightly (or toasted) more than the traditional pale malts, giving the Vienna-style beer a toasted malt quality. The spices and ancho chili in the recado are also toasted. The potato-celery root has a crisp toasted crust, and, as mentioned earlier, Vienna-style lagers are perfect with spicy food.

Commercial examples of a Mexican Vienna style lager are Negra Modelo, Dos Equis, and Indio Oscura.

PORK TENDERLOIN

MICKY DOWD

ALDEN COUNTRY INN, LYME, NH

I think a pork dish is best for beer and food pairing. We do have one—a tenderloin of pork **(Pan Roasted Pork Tenderloin)** that we serve with a mango chutney sauce, and that works real well with beer for me.

What is important in pairing is that you have to like the beer. People know what beers they like and what foods they like. I think that it is something that you don't have to overthink. A person who drinks Budweiser has that ideal, you shouldn't try to serve a Catamount with his dinner and expect it to work better than his Budweiser.

I try to do things that people can expect to find on the menu when they come back. My idea is to promote the restaurant as well as the beers. The philosophy we have here as far as our food is to promote traditional New England cuisine. For a while we carried sort of a traditional bar menu and a more sophisticated dining room menu. More people were interested in the bar menu, so we now do a more "middle-of-the-road" menu where we keep it simple and traditional.

SAUSAGES, ONIONS, AND APPLES

DAVID MILLIGAN

BRICKTOWN BREWERY, OKLAHOMA CITY, OK

We have a sausage plate **(Three Sausages with Caramelized Onions and Apples)** that has three kinds of sausage; chicken apple sausage, andouille, and bratwurst. Fresh hand-made sausages are best if you have them. We serve it with Copperhead-caramelized onions and apples. We use Copperhead with balsamic vinegar and brown sugar and caramelize the apples and onions in that. It is a real nice concept because you get the bitter from the beer and sweet from the sugar. The bitter flavor comes from reducing the beer.

BARBECUE

Finally, there is one notion that needs to be cleared up: What, exactly, is "barbecue"?

The accurate use of the word "barbecue" is as a description of a grill, pit, or outdoor fireplace for roasting meats. The word comes from the American Spanish word *barbacoa*, from the Haitian Creole word for a framework set on posts. The origin of that word is, from a word of a similar meaning from the Tiano, an extinct aboriginal tribe of Arawakan Indian people of the West Indies. From Europe there is also a suggestion that the origin of the word is from the French "de la barbe a la queue" (from the beard to the tail), referring to the appearance of the animal impaled on the roasting spit. As the French influence in the southern United States, especially in Louisiana, the true origin of the word is probably intertwined to the point of never being determined. So much the better! This opens the door to all kinds of lively arguments about what "real" barbecue is. There is some talk of smoked meats as being the only "true" barbecue. Then there is the equally lively debate on the heritage of the tomato-based or vinegar-based barbecue sauce. All of this makes for some fine eating.

No matter which technique, or sauce, you subscribe to, the primal rhythms involved in cooking over an open fire is echoed in the history of brewing beer.

SAUCE AND RUB

CHEF DAN RUSSO

VIRGIL'S REAL BBQ, NEW YORK, NY

After much research, Chef Dan Russo can assure us that "There are two essentials to proper barbecue; the "sauce" and the "rub". There is also the question of whether to add the flavor to the meat before or after presentation."

Russo notes that there are major differences to how barbecue is prepared in the major barbecue regions of the United States. "In Kansas City they rub a mixture of spices and peppers on the meat before it is cooked. Carolina, east and west, is divided by smoke or grilled. In Oklahoma "barbecue" is always over an open grill. Then there are discussions about "hot" and "cold" smoking, pits or open-flame. All pits are different—some have a furnace that drives it and large door. The "pit" style barbecue needs to be tended by a "pit master," who must turn the coals and the meat, all night in many cases."

CHAPTER 9

Salads

ANDY FINESTONE
BOSCOS, GERMANTOWN, TN

We had four course meal…We did steamed cockles, in a cream ale…then a fruit salad with the tropical fruit dressing, served with a wheat beer.

Here is where beer has it all over wine. That bowl of incredibly tiny leaves, just kissed with a hint of lemon juice and herbed vinegar will lay waste to the simple vin ordinare and blitzkrieg a fine wine. You see, vinegar and wine do not mix. The taste buds get very rattled and the flavors of the wine take on almost unpleasant tones. This does not happen with beer. Many simple vinaigrettes can be improved by adding a splash of beer.

CHEF SEAN WOODS
RITZ CARLTON ON AMELIA ISLAND, AMELIA ISLAND, FL

For the last Sam Adams dinner, we served their Cherry Wheat beer and made a seviche with the Cherry Wheat beer and citric and cooked the salmon in the beer and citric and used the liquid from the seviche to make a vinaigrette. Between the alcohol and the citrus the lemon, lime and orange also helped…with the beer and citrus to cook it and we tossed it in a nice field green salad with baby greens, goat cheese, fresh cherries, and jicama and dicon for a crunch, and julienned the salmon and tossed it in there. We actually could have made an entree out of this. It was very simple. Between the fresh cherries and the cherry wheat beer it came out very nice.

Cherry Wheat makes an excellent vinaigrette. It is light and refreshing. It makes a great summertime entrée salad for lunch. In fact, I am going to use that as an entrée salad here in a few weeks. I am thinking about the late fall and winter menu and trying to think of what I can do with the apples that are going to be coming in season.

There are times when a delicate salad of baby greens falls flat. These are times that call for hearty, even savory, salads. One of the basic salads in any kitchen is the potato salad. This summer favorite can come dressed either in mayonnaise or oil and vinegar. The following is a salad that goes well with beer for a few reasons. The slightly malty flavor of the beer complements the bacon flavors, the hops refresh the palate and the cool liquid prepares the eater with a refreshing pause to wipe the sand from the side of the plate, check out the scene, or have another sip of beer. Jeff Schagrin, of Stuart, Florida, has a special place in his heart for warm weather and lots of customers buying the fixings for picnics.

JEFF SCHAGRIN
HARBOR BAY GOURMET, STUART, FL

From there we go to the salads—we offer chicken, Caesar, and Greek salads, pasta salads, and we are famous for our **Harbor Bay Gourmet French Potato Salad.** These are also sold at retail and we feature some of them as specials in the restaurant.

We have one of the most outstanding potato salads in the world. People come from all over to buy our salad. It has new potatoes, scallions, bacon, and it goes really well with ale.

CHAPTER 10
Breads and Cheeses

CHEF JOHN GALLICHAN

SWANS BREWPUB/BUCKERFIELD'S BREWERY, VICTORIA, B.C., CANADA

(The Buckerfield Brewery is part of a bed & breakfast inn and restaurant facing Victoria's picturesque harbor.)

We are a smaller brew pub. We feature Swan's Beer Bread. I think our beer bread is unique because we use our own stout. Customers, and comments in the local newspaper, have noted how it has its own special flavor, almost like a sour dough. It is a basic yeast based bread, very simple, with only four ingredients.

One thing we do that goes over very well is the beer-bread calzone. What I do is take our beer bread recipe, cut it down to a quarter the size, and use that to make the calzone pizza, or a beer-bread pizza. We can do so many things with that beer-bread recipe.

BEER YEAST ROLLS

CHEF RICHARD HAMILTON

BIG RIVER GRILLE & BREWING WORKS, CHATTANOOGA, TN

I really like the yeast corn and honey roll. I really like it! I think it's light…You think it is a corn bread but it isn't. It's a yeast roll and what makes you think it's a corn bread is the stoutness of the beer we use. We use a stout in there with sweet white and yellow corn—whole kernels and some pureed.…I like to go out to the bar and enjoy those rolls as something to go with a good beer. They have a sweet taste, but they also have a savory taste. You get the best of both worlds. As I say, it is a very simple recipe. People love bread—it is very comforting and at the same time "sexy."

RUSSIAN BLACK BREAD

DELMAR CRIM

EMPIRE BREWING CO., SYRACUSE, NY

We make a really excellent **Russian Black Bread** that we use for our sardine sandwich with red onion and cream cheese served with the stout. The bread in itself is a meal. We have a baker who comes in at night who I trained. The bread is an old family recipe. You throw it all together, bake in a low oven. It takes forever but it is so moist, and it is the best bread I have made.

CHEESE

JEROME C. DENYS

LECHEVAL BLANC, MONTREAL, QUEBEC, CANADA

Jerome C. Denys, the brewer at LeCheval Blanc, a snug microbrewery and simple pub in Montreal, believes that good beer should be enjoyed with good friends, good conversation, and simple foods.

We have an especially strong Canadian cheddar cheese made up in the Lac St. Jean area. We have to have it shipped to us by messenger. This guy is funny. He makes most of his cheese for England—apparently it is one of the Queen's favorite cheeses, but is unknown here in Montreal. We have it here though, and serve it at the tavern. **I must say that a strong cheddar cheese is one of the best simple foods to go with our kind of beers.** Especially my beers. They are free fermented in bottles, like a Belgian beer, and they are very strong ales.

CHAPTER 11

Desserts

Beer is not often thought of as something to have for dessert, especially after a five- or six-course meal. By itself, it is an excellent digestive, and it also adds a new flavor dimension to everything from ice cream to cake. The opportunity to combine flavors, especially contrasting the dry flavor of beer with the traditional sweet flavors of desserts, can be a lot of fun.

First in line are the beers that can be served instead of a traditional after-dinner drink. The Swiss brew Samichlaus Bier, brewed only on December 6th (St. Nicholas Day in Switzerland) is aged for a full year before it is bottled. The result is a dark, rich, highly alcoholic brew (14.9% by volume) that has been called "the world's strongest lager" by many beer experts. Although it is a lager, this beer should be stored and served at cellar temperature (50°F) in order to fully appreciate its flavor and aroma. It goes especially well with dense chocolate desserts such as flourless chocolate cake, chocolate petite fours or, as it is offered by Sam Barbarie at both of his Waterfront Alehouse locations in New York City, with chocolate popcorn.

Beer can also be used in traditional desserts as a substitute for something in the recipe that calls for a coffee, chocolate, or toasty flavor. Chef Joe Kubik, of John Harvard's, in Cambridge, MA, creates his "hot fudge sauce" from scratch. Instead of using coffee to enhance the richness and flavor of the sauce, he uses a stout beer. "We make our fudge sauce from scratch. Since most fudge sauces call for coffee, I just substituted stout. When I look at the quantity of sauce we use, I would have to say that we now have a great fudge sauce at this point," says Kubik.

Chef Michel Notredame, from Cuve Notredame in Philadelphia, PA, suggests that simple desserts that bring out the best of fruit and beer can be the perfect coda to any meal,

I ran out of dessert one day and I remembered being in France with a family that were friends of mine, and none of us were big on dessert. We were ending a bottle of excellent burgundy and I thought that we should just drink it but they said they would cut up strawberries, add a little sugar to the berries, and pour the leftover wine over the berries in a glass for dessert. They told me that they did that all the time. I said it was a shame to use such a good wine but they told me, "The better the wine, the better the dessert!" After tasting it I couldn't disagree with them at all. It is the same thing with beer. If you have a good fruit beer added to fresh berries…You see I had a big party here one day and ran out of dessert. I did have Kriek Boon on draft and just cut up the fresh berries that I had on hand, put some of them in a glass, and poured the cherry beer on top of them—it was fantastic.

Other desserts that can use unique substitutions in their flavor are cakes. Baking with beer also adds a special leavening character to the dessert. Clark Nickerson, chef at The Granite Brewery in Toronto, Ontario, Canada, bakes an **Irish Stout Cake** that includes Guinness Stout. The result is a cake that has a unique combination of spice, coffee, and malt flavor. Chef Nickerson suggests icing the cake with a cream cheese icing for a slightly rich finish to a meal.

If ethnic treasures adapted to the beer theme is something you are looking for, I would suggest the **"Beeramisu"** created by Bill Kunz in his kitchen at Growler's Pub, in St. Louis, MO. His use of a porter-style beer instead of the traditional brandy creates a slightly dry counterpoint to the sweet essence of the rich Italian dessert. The rich flavor of the porter is even more pleasing than the heavier version using brandy.

CHOCOLATE IMPERIAL STOUT MOUSSE

EXECUTIVE CHEF ANGELO J. GIORDANO
OLD BAY RESTAURANT, NEW BRUNSWICK, NJ

As far as things that surprised me, and one of the things that I am most proud of, was the time that Garret Oliver came from Brooklyn Brewing and he had just released his Black Chocolate Stout. I thought, well, it has "chocolate" in the name, I'll bet I can make a chocolate mousse with this beer. So I got this new product that is on the market. It has chocolate and has finely ground espresso beans in the chocolate. So I thought that the coffee and the chocolate overtones in the stout would match well. With a little experimenting with my basic chocolate mousse recipe, I came up with what I called **Brooklyn Chocolate Imperial Stout Mousse.** Oliver gave me very high marks on that particular pairing.

AFTER DINNER

CHEF MICHELLE BEALE
DOCK STREET RESTAURANT, WASHINGTON D.C.

Chef Beale enjoys the whole range of craft brews with her passion—single-malt Scotch.

I drink single malts with a beer back. I 'm very much into pairing single malts with beer. It is fantastic. A 16-year-old Talisker with a Scottish ale is a flavor combination that is hard to improve on. It is like when you put a couple of drops of water in a single malt to oxidize it. I take a sip of my scotch and a sip of my beer and let it BE in my mouth…it's wonderful.

PART

2

THE
RECIPES

Mise en Place

The following recipes are those recipes that every cook knows by heart. They are so basic that many cookbooks assume their readers know what they consist of and how to use them in more complex recipes. They are presented here in order that experienced cooks can refresh their culinary memory, and new cooks can get a handle on some basics of cooking.

The *mise en place* is a French phrase that, roughly translated, means "getting all your stuff in a row." With all your ingredients prepared, and all the pots, pans, knives, whisks, and spoons you will need to prepare a certain dish close at hand, a cook can concentrate on the preparation of the dishes for a dinner without any time wasted or procedure unnecessary duplicated. Many of the *mise en place* are combinations of herbs and spices that are used as basic building blocks to build to a more complex dish. These combinations, such as curry powder, chili powder, Chinese five spice, and bouquet garni, can be purchased premixed in a grocery store, but add so much more depth and personal touch to your dishes when you prepare them yourself. Other *mise en place* are procedures that lead to the preparation of dishes. These procedures are making a basic roux, and preparing four basic stocks: "brown," "white," fish, and chicken (not to forget vegetable).

In some cases the recipe may call for "parts" of ingredients. This simply means that you take a basic "part" and give it volume or weight (you can use either). Make that one "part" either a tablespoon, teaspoon, ounce, or "handful". The only trick here is to keep all the "parts" equal. One cup holds a lot more olive oil than it does olives. This puts the problem of deciding how to measure one "part" olive oil and one "part" flour in perspective. (Spoon measurements are advised for the previous illustration.) Measurements are meant as guidelines, not absolutes. It is often more important to understand why you are using certain ingredient combinations than to use an exact measurement. The following "recipes" are a basic selection of Mise en Place that should be a part of every cook's repertoire.

Mirepoix

Almost every roast, braise, or boil calls for something called a mirepoix or a bouquet garni. This is where many will close the book and remember that it has been a long time since they have gone out for dinner at their favorite restaurant. The following will dispel the mystery of the mirepoix and bouquet garni.

A mirepoix is a set of basic vegetable flavors that are added to a recipe. Cut in uniform pieces they release the optimum amount of flavor into the dish. Always use the freshest ingredients.

> two parts onions, chopped
>
> one part carrots, chopped
>
> one part celery, chopped

Chop the vegetables into pieces of equal size (approximately one half of an inch). These diced vegetables will be adding a slightly sweet, slightly grassy, very distinct flavor to the dish.

Add this mixture to recipe in quantities and at the appropriate time called for in the recipe.

Bouquet Garni

1	sprig fresh thyme
3	parsley stems
2	$3/4$-inch sections of celery stalk
1	bay leaf

Place the thyme, parsley, and bay leaf in the hollow of one piece of celery, place the other piece of celery over that assembly and tie together with string. Leave in the dish while cooking only until the right flavor has been added. Taste every 15 minutes or so to determine when you should remove the bundle.

Basic Roux

A roux is a mixture of flour and fats or oils that is the base for many sauces and gravies. The essential measurement is one part oil to one part flour. The amount of time that you cook the flour and oil mixture depends on how dark a sauce you want to make. Cheese sauces and white binding sauces need to be cooked only until the flour just absorbs the oil. Gumbo roux should be cooked just to this side of burning. The procedure is relatively simple, but the control of the process determines the success of the finished dish.

Almost all roux begins with the addition of rendered fat, butter, or oil to a pot. When roasting meat, the pan juices can be used to start the roux. Stir the equal amount of flour into the hot oil. Stir quickly over a medium flame. The object is to cook the flour and oil to the point that the sauce will not taste like a flour and water paste. The minimum time is 5 minutes. Once the flour is cooked, you can adjust the heat to begin to brown the mixture. This is where the range of sauces begin, from lightest egg shell white to almost ebony. Once the roux has reached the color you want, it is time to add the liquids called for in the recipe. Follow the recipe to completion.

Stocks

If the roux is the essential of a sauce, then the stock is the soul of the sauce. The quality of the stock significantly effects the quality of the dish. Since most of us have rather busy schedules, the immediate answer is canned, or tinned, broth. Excellent products are on the shelves. Make sure you choose the low salt or no-salt products. It is easy enough to add salt to a sauce rather than take it out.

With a refrigerator full of leftovers, the idea of a stock can be inspiring. The key to a clear stock is to skim the surface of all the "nasty stuff" and cook at just a simmer. This will release all the essential flavors from the food you have in the pot.

STOCK BASICS

(a) For a brown stock, roast the carcass or bones in a 350°F oven until well browned. This will result in more flavor in the stock.

(b) For a fish stock, there is no need to roast the bones or shells. It is a good idea to sauté them briefly to bring out their flavor.

(c) Start with just enough water to cover the stock basics (bones, shells, etc.). Maintain the simmer for about $1/2$ hour for fish and for up to 3 hours for brown stock.

(d) Keep at least one large tin of chicken stock and one large tin of beef stock in your pantry.

Basic Pastry

Pastry dough is used to make pies and to top stews. It is especially important to know how to make a good pastry dough.

Many professional chefs call basic pastry dough "3-2-1 Dough." This is because it is made from three parts flour, two parts fat, and one part water (by weight).

2	cups all-purpose flour
6	ounces chilled unsalted butter
$\frac{1}{2}$	cup chilled vegetable shortening
$\frac{1}{2}$	cup ice water

Cut the butter and shortening into the flour with a pastry cutter. Continue until the texture is similar to coarsely ground meal. Stir in the water with a fork. When the dough forms a sticky ball, add the last of the flour and it should form a less sticky ball. Now, and only for as short a time as necessary, use your hands to blend the flour, shortening/butter, and water into an compact, smooth, relatively elastic ball. Flatten slightly to a circle about 2 inches thick. Wrap in plastic wrap and refrigerate for at least 2 hours.

Just before you need it, take the dough out and place it on a well-floured work surface. Use a rolling pin to roll the dough to a sheet approximately $\frac{1}{8}$ inch thick. Lift the sheet of dough on the length of the rolling pin and place the dish you want to use the pastry on upon your work surface. Lower the sheet of dough on the dish and prepare as instructed in your recipe.

Spices

Spices and herbs should be as fresh as possible. There are certain mixtures sold in stores called chili powder, curry powder, and Chinese five spice mix. The following recipes are spice combinations that can be adjusted to your taste to produce a chili, curry, or Szechwan Chicken dish that is unique yet to style.

CHILI POWDER

1½	tablespoon chili peppers, dried and ground
½	tablespoon cumin
½	teaspoon oregano, dried
¼	teaspoon garlic powder
⅛	teaspoon coriander, ground

Place all spices in a spice mill and grind together. Store in an airtight jar and use as directed in your recipe. **(YIELDS 2½ TABLESPOONS)**

CHINESE FIVE SPICE

1	tablespoon star anise
1	tablespoon cloves
1	tablespoon Szechwan pepper
1	tablespoon fennel seeds
1	tablespoon cinnamon

Grind the spices together in a spice mill and keep in a small airtight container. Use as called for in recipes. **(YIELDS 5 TABLESPOONS)**

CURRY POWDER

3	tablespoons cumin seeds
1	tablespoon coriander seeds
½	teaspoon mustard seeds
4	dried chilies (to taste)
1	teaspoon cinnamon (ground)
1	tablespoon tumeric (ground)
1	teaspoon ginger (ground)

Roast all seeds and chilies in a preheated 300°F degrees oven for about 5 minutes. Remove and separate the chilies. Let the seeds stay warm and, wearing food gloves, remove the seeds from the chilies. Return the chilies to the seed and spice mixture and grind together in a spice mill. Store in an airtight container. Use as directed in a recipe.

Brewer's Breakfast

JOHN DICKENSON, WYNKOOP BREWING, DENVER, CO

    Eat this and you will gain much strength, vigor, and stamina.

1   bowl of granola

1   cup fresh hot unhopped wort

1/2   cup fresh fruit, your choice

1   cup plain yogurt

Fill your breakfast bowl with granola. Pour desired amount of hot wort straight from mash, combine, and garnish with fresh fruit and/or plain yogurt.

SERVES 1

Spicy Cheese and Lager Dip

CHEF ANDREW LASSETER, HEARTLAND BREWERY, NYC

 Use Velveeta™ cheese for a faultless smooth texture. (Do not tell your gourmet friends!)

1 pound jalapeño Jack cheese, chopped or shredded

1 pound yellow cheddar or Velveeta™ cheese, chopped or shredded

1 plum tomato, seeded and diced

1 tablespoon chopped fresh cilantro

4 ounces lager

Place the cheeses and beer in a double boiler. When the cheese has melted, stir in the tomato and cilantro.

Serve with tortilla or corn chips.

SERVES 6–8

PARKER HOUSE INN

Black Olive Tapenade

CHEF BARBARA FORRESTER,
PARKER HOUSE INN, QUECHEE, VERMONT

1   cup black olives, dry-cured, pitted
1   teaspoon chopped garlic
¼   cup capers
½   teaspoon hot pepper flakes
1   tablespoon rum
¼–⅓ cup olive oil

Combine all ingredients, except oil, in a food processor. Process until finely chopped, but not pureed. Add enough oil for desired consistency.

SERVES 6 AS AN APPETIZER

White Bean and Tasso Soup

CHEF JACK SEDIVY,
SILO MICROBREWERY, LOUISVILLE, KY

 Note: Tasso is a highly seasoned pork mixture.

8 cups onion, chopped
1¼ pounds tasso, sliced fine
2½ cups garlic, minced
½ cup scallions
2 gallons white beans
1 gallon amber beer
2 gallons chicken stock
1 cup Creole mustard
2 tablespoons Tabasco sauce
Salt and pepper to taste

In a large stock/soup pot, sauté onions, scallions, tasso, and garlic. Add remaining ingredients. Simmer approximately 4 hours. (Add liquid if necessary.) Season to taste

SERVES 12

Pizza Kitchen & Brewery

Stone Beer Cheese Soup

ANDY FINESTONE, BOSCOS, GERMANTOWN, TN

1   medium onion, chopped

2   stalks celery, chopped

1   red bell pepper, chopped

5   strips smoked bacon

¼   cup olive oil

2   quarts chicken stock

1   pint stone beer

2   cups heavy cream

1   teaspoon fresh thyme

2   tablespoons Tabasco sauce

1   tablespoon Worcestershire sauce
    Salt and pepper to taste

8   ounces sharp yellow cheddar
    cheese

2   ounces blue cheese

Sauté onion, celery, pepper, and bacon in olive oil. Drain off the oils and add stock, beer, and cream. Bring just to a boil. Add the remaining ingredients. If necessary, you can thicken with a mixture of 1 tablespoon of firm butter combined with 1 tablespoon of flour.

SERVES 6

Summer Porter Chowder

THE INN AT
MAPLEWOOD FARM

CHEF LAURA SIMOES
THE INN AT MAPLEWOOD FARM, HILLSBOROUGH, NH

This is a vegetarian alternative to chowders made with chicken stock. This is an ideal soup for a hearty luncheon or supper entree. Serve with Butter Crust Beer Bread.

2	tablespoon olive oil
1	small onion, chopped
4	scallions, chopped
1	zucchini squash, sliced into thin round shapes
1	summer squash, sliced into thin round shapes
3	ears of corn (remove kernels and reserve)
6	ounces Catamount Porter
4	cups whole milk
½	cup heavy cream
	Salt and pepper to taste

Heat the olive oil in a deep fry pan over medium high heat. Sauté the onion and scallions until nearly soft. Add the zucchini and summer squash and sauté for about 5 minutes or until al dente. Add the corn kernels and porter. Stirring occasionally, cook over medium heat until the liquid is absorbed/evaporated. (This vegetable mixture may be served as it is. It makes enough for 4–6 servings as a side dish.) Put the vegetable/porter mixture in a blender or food processor and puree. Add the milk slowly while blending and then return the chowder to the heavy pot. While reheating over a low flame, stir in the heavy cream and add the salt and pepper.

SERVES 4

Wynkoop's Gorgonzola Ale Soup

JOHN DICKENSON, WYNKOOP BREWING, DENVER, CO

2   pounds red potatoes, peeled and coarsely chopped

1   medium yellow onion, peeled and coarsely chopped

2   quarts water

4   ounces Gorgonzola cheese

1   12-ounce bottle Railyard Ale

2   cups chicken broth

1   cup heavy cream or half-and-half

2   teaspoons salt

1   teaspoon ground white pepper

Place potatoes and onions in medium saucepan with water and bring to a boil. Simmer until potatoes are completely soft, about 45 minutes.

Strain potatoes and reserve water. Allow potatoes to cool slightly and purée in a food processor, adding reserved potato water as needed until mixture is very smooth.

Return to heat and add remaining ingredients. Stir until Gorgonzola is melted.

Serve with a hearty beer bread or a crusty loaf of French bread.

VARIATIONS: Use smoked Gouda or pepper Jack cheese instead of Gorgonzola.

For a lower fat version, use vegetable stock instead of chicken stock and whole or skim milk instead of cream. Thicken with a little cornstarch dissolved in water.

SERVES 8

Andouille Sausage, Clam, and Mussel Stew

CHEF ANDREW LASSETER, HEARTLAND BREWERY, NYC

   A fine party dish

1	large andouille sausage, diced
1	tablespoon chopped garlic
1	large white onion, diced
4	stalks celery, diced
1	teaspoon fresh thyme leaves
1	red pepper, diced
1	cup clam juice
1	cup crushed plum tomatoes
4	ounces lager beer
2	dozen littleneck clams
2	pounds mussels
	Salt and pepper to taste

In a 4-quart pot sauté the sausage until brown and some of the fat has rendered. Add the garlic and sauté until slightly brown. Add the onion, celery, thyme, and red pepper and sauté together until softened. Add the clam juice and crushed tomatoes and bring to a boil. Simmer for 5 minutes. Add the lager and return to a boil. Add clams and mussels and simmer, covered, until the shellfish are opened

Serve in bowls with a basket of crusty bread for dipping. Beer suggestions: Rolling Rock or any other pale American lager-style beer

SERVES 4 AS A LIGHT DINNER OR 8 AS AN APPETIZER

Shrimp Shell Soup

CORY MATTSON, FEARRINGTON HOUSE, PITTSBORO, NC

FEARRINGTON H·O·U·S·E

Frugality and basics are the keys to this tasty dish. The best beer to use is a dark, rich-flavored ale. The rich color and sweet malt flavor reduce perfectly in this case. Don't worry about the hops–the heat of the peppers and the stock marry the bitter and heat nicely.

Shrimp shells (leftover or frozen) (enough to half fill your Dutch oven.)

6   tablespoons olive oil
1   teaspoon red pepper flakes
1   teaspoon fresh thyme
1   teaspoon green peppercorns
3   bay leaves
1   12-ounce bottle of ale, rich, dark
1   small onion, peeled and finely diced
4   celery stalks, finely diced
1   stem leeks, peeled and finely diced
1   small ginger bulb, chopped
½   gallon chicken broth (enough to cover shells)

GARNISH
½   cup cooked shrimp, chopped
½   cup scallions, sliced
½   cup assorted mushrooms, chopped
4   tablespoons soy sauce (approximate)
2   tablespoons sesame oil (approximate)
    Salt and pepper to taste

Heat a Dutch oven. Sweat the shells, olive oil, red pepper, thyme, peppercorns, and bay leaves until very orange and light brown (approximately 10 minutes). Add the ale and simmer until it is evaporated (approximately 10 minutes). Add onion, celery, leek, and ginger. Cover with broth. Simmer 30 minutes. Strain, add garnish. Remember, light garnish will float and heavy garnish will fall to the bottom of the bowl. This effect creates a multilayer dish. Experiment with garnishes until you find just what you enjoy most. Season to taste with soy sauce, sesame oil, and salt and pepper.

SERVES 4

Poached Striped Sea Bass
with Spicy Red Pepper Cream Sauce

CHEF WADE SIMPSON, LANTANA GRILLE, PHOENIX, AZ

BOUILLON

5 cups water

6 bay leaves

1 lemon, cut in half

1 lime, cut in half

10 peppercorns

1 bunch (five stalks) parsley stems

10 Saaz hops flowers

4 leaves green parts of leeks

CARAMELIZED LEEKS

2 leeks, cored, sliced into 1½-inch pieces, and washed

1 tablespoon unsalted butter

2 tablespoon sugar

½ cup cream

SPICY RED PEPPER SAUCE

1 tablespoon olive oil

1 red pepper, seeded and chopped roughly

1 clove garlic, chopped

1 teaspoon red chilies, crushed

2 cups cream

Salt and pepper

6 fillets striped sea bass (6-ounce portion per person)

1 bottle St. Landelin Blond Abbey Ale

4 cups court bouillon

1 cup caramelized leeks

1 cup red pepper sauce

Combine all the bouillon ingredients in pot and simmer for 20–30 minutes. Strain and keep warm. Before use, add 1 teaspoon salt.

In a sauté pan, sauté the leeks in butter on medium heat for 5 minutes. Add the sugar and stir in until sugar dissolves. As the sugar starts to boil, add cream and let cook one minute. Remove from heat and keep warm.

In a sauce pot, heat the olive oil on medium heat. Add the red pepper, garlic, shallots, and chilies. Stir occasionally with a wooden spoon for 3 to 5 minutes. Add cream, bring to a boil and let simmer for 5 to 10 minutes. Place in a blender, blend well, and strain through a fine strainer. Keep warm.

In a baking dish, place sea bass skin side up. Pour St. Landelin Blond Ale over fish. Let marinate in refrigerator for at least 2 hours. When ready to cook, preheat oven to 400°F. Add enough court bouillon to baking dish with fish to heat beer. Place in oven and cook until skin is able to pull away from meat, about 10 minutes. Remove from oven and remove sea bass from poaching liquid. In center of each plate, spoon some leeks, place sea bass over leeks, and place sauce around bass. Garnish dish with a steamed vegetable and either herbed rice or beans.

SERVES 6

Ale-Battered Cod with Red Chili Tartar Sauce

BRICKTOWN BREWERY
R E S T A U R A N T

DAVID MILLIGAN,
BRICKTOWN BREWERY, OKLAHOMA CITY, OK

Chef Milligan suggests, "Use the freshest fish you can get. If you can't get cod, you can use halibut. Delicate portions of fish may fall apart with this preparation."

1½ pounds cod fillet
2   bottles amber ale
3   cups tempura flour
4   inches of canola oil in a Dutch oven

RED CHILI TARTAR SAUCE

2   cups mayonnaise
¼   cup sweet pickle relish
¼   cup dill pickle relish
1   tablespoon yellow onion, minced
1   tablespoon lemon juice
2   tablespoons Louisiana red hot sauce

Cut cod into 2-ounce chunks. Thoroughly combine room temperature ale with tempura flour. Drop fish into batter and coat thoroughly. Heat the oil until a small cube of bread quickly browns. Transfer into frying oil and cook until medium brown (approximately 7 minutes). Transfer fried fish one piece at a time so they don't stick together. Place fish on paper towels to drain off excess oil. Serve with deep-fried potatoes and **Red Chili Tartar Sauce.**

SERVES 4

Moroccan Halibut with Pilsner Butter

CHEF MICHAEL PERSELAY,
TRIUMPH BREWING CO., PRINCETON, NJ

 Prepare the curry oil at least 24 hours in advance.

CURRY OIL

1   tablespoon curry powder

½   cup canola oil

SPICE MIX

½   tablespoon cumin seed

½   tablespoon coriander seed

½   tablespoon fennel seed

¼   tablespoon black peppercorns

4   6 ounce halibut fillets

HUMMUS

1   small onion

2   garlic cloves

1   fresh cayenne pepper

1   15-ounce can garbanzo beans, drained

    Salt and pepper to taste

¼   cup olive oil

PILSNER BUTTER

¼   cup pilsner beer

1   tablespoon honey (if needed)

4   ounces unsalted sweet butter

    Salt and pepper to taste

Toast the curry powder in a hot pan then add oil. Remove from heat and store in an airtight glass container. *Let stand 24 hours before using.*

Toast the spices in a hot pan, until golden. Remove from heat and crush between two sheets of wax paper with a rolling pin.

Preheat the oven to 375°F. Place the halibut in a bowl. Add enough curry oil to coat fish. Sprinkle the spice mix over the fish on both sides. Sear the fish over high heat, finish in the oven at 375°F for approximately 8 minutes, for medium done.

In a food processor "pulse chop" the onion, garlic, and cayenne. Add the garbanzo beans and pulse chop until coarse. Add salt and pepper. Continue to pulse chop until just incorporated. *Do not puree.*

In a pan, reduce the pilsner by half. Take off heat. If the pilsner reduction is too bitter, before adding butter, add 1 tablespoon honey, reduce again. Whisk in butter and salt and pepper. Save in airtight glass or metal container

Place the hummus in the center of the plate. Cut each piece of fish corner to corner and arrange around hummus. Drizzle butter sauce over fish Drizzle an equal portion of curry oil. Garnish with chopped chives and diced tomatoes.

SERVES 4

Mussels in Belgian Ale

SAM BARBIERI,
WATERFRONT ALE HOUSE, BROOKLYN, NY

     This is a great summer appetizer served with a pale ale.

2	shallots, diced fine
2	tablespoons olive oil
½	cup fennel bulbs, sliced thin
1	quart mussels, cleaned
8	ounces Belgian ale (white or pale)
1	plum tomato, peeled, seeded, and chopped
2	teaspoons lemongrass, chopped
1	bay leaf
2	tablespoons garlic butter
½	lime, juice only
	Salt and pepper

Sauté shallots in olive oil until transparent. Add fennel and sauté until slightly soft. Add mussels and ale and bring to a boil. Add tomato, lemongrass, and bay leaf. Lower heat, cover, and cook until mussels open. Remove mussels to a large bowl and keep warm. Return broth to a boil and whisk in the garlic butter and lime juice. Season broth to taste with salt and pepper. Pour sauce over mussels.

Serve with crusty French bread and a Belgian ale.

SERVES 6

Baked Salmon with Hefe-Weizen, Sweet Corn, and Fennel

JOHN DICKENSON, WYNKOOP BREWING, DENVER, CO

The spicy flavors of hefe-weizen and fresh fennel are contrasted by the richness of the salmon and butter and the sweetness of the corn.

3	ounces (3/4 stick) whole sweet butter, cut into 1-ounce pieces
6	8-ounce salmon fillets
	Salt and pepper to taste
2	cups of hefe-weizen style beer (Wixa Weiss, Tabernash Heffe, or Paulaner Hefe)
2	ears of fresh sweet corn
1	medium red bell pepper, julienne
1	bulb fresh fennel, julienne
1	bunch green onions, bias cut into 1-inch pieces

Preheat oven to 350°F. Melt 1 ounce of butter and brush salmon fillets. Season fillets with salt and pepper and put in a baking dish large enough to hold the fillets without crowding. Pour the cup of beer around, not over, fillets. Bake in preheated oven for 10–15 minutes depending upon thickness of fillets (remember—10 minutes for every 1 inch of thickness). Meanwhile, remove kernels from ears of corn with a sharp knife. Melt 1 ounce of butter in a large skillet or sauté pan. Add corn, pepper, and fennel and sauté over high heat for about 5 minutes. Season with salt and pepper. Add remaining cup of beer and simmer vegetable mixture for another 5 minutes until corn and fennel are tender. Remove salmon from the oven and pour any remaining juices into the corn mixture; finish corn mixture with 1 ounce of butter and toss in the green onions.

Place salmon on serving plate and spoon an even amount of the corn mixture over the filets.

VARIATIONS: Feel free to broil or grill the salmon, but you will need to baste the fish with beer.

SERVES 6

Norwegian Salmon Fillet in Honey Porter

DENIS MANNEVILLE, WEBERS, BALTIMORE, MD

MARINADE

2   12-ounce bottles of Honey Porter

4   cloves crushed garlic

1   bunch fresh dill, chopped

4   sprigs fresh thyme, chopped

1   serrano chili pepper

6   tablespoons olive oil

     White pepper and sea salt to taste

4   8-ounce fresh fillets of salmon

TERIYAKI GLAZE

$^3/_4$ cup apricot glaze

$^1/_2$ cup teriyaki sauce

VIN-BLANC SAUCE

$^1/_2$ cup white wine

$^3/_4$ cup fish stock

$^1/_4$ cup heavy cream

Combine all the marinade ingredients in a baking platter and place the salmon in the platter. Marinate for 6 hours. Remove the salmon. Pour the marinade in a baking pan and warm it just to a pre-boil. Add the salmon and poach for 6–8 minutes. Prepare the teriyaki glaze by combining apricot glaze and teriyaki sauce in a saucepan. Bring to a boil and reduce until the glaze coats the spoon. Put aside.

Prepare the vin-blanc sauce by placing the wine in a saucepan and bringing to a boil. Then add the fish stock. Reduce to about half the initial volume. Remove from heat and add the cream. Reserve the sauce in a warm place.

Place the teriyaki glaze on a plate, place a piece of salmon in the middle of the plate. Using a spoon, drizzle the vin blanc sauce around the salmon, on the teriyaki glaze, to create a contrasting pattern.

SERVES 4

OCEANA
RESTAURANT

Salmon Tartare
Wrapped with Smoked Salmon

CHEF RICK MOONEN, OCEANA, NYC

3   egg yolks

3   teaspoons Dijon mustard

1½ tablespoons fresh lemon juice

1½ tablespoons fresh lime juice

3   tablespoons fish sauce (available at Oriental food markets)

4   tablespoons shallots, peeled and diced

4   tablespoons chopped capers

1½ teaspoons Tabasco sauce

¾   cup virgin olive oil

1½ pounds sushi-quality salmon (preferably from the belly), skinned and diced

1   cup soy oil

1   cup chives, chopped

1   cup parsley, chopped

1   teaspoon fresh tarragon

½   teaspoon ground white pepper

6   slices smoked salmon, sliced into 1-inch wide ribbons

     Sevruga caviar for garnish (optional)

6   slices white bread

6   ounces pea shoots, dressed with lemon juice, olive oil, salt, and pepper

First, create an emulsified (mayonnaise-style) sauce to bind the salmon and flavor the tartare. Whip together the egg yolks, mustard, lemon and lime juices, fish sauce, diced shallot, capers, and Tabasco. Add the oil drop by drop at first, whisking the mixture vigorously until the oil begins to incorporate into the mixture. Then, pour the oil in a slow stream while constantly mixing until the sauce is finished. Taste for seasonings (lemon juice, fish sauce, and pepper) and adjust.

Spoon about half of the sauce into a bowl and add the diced salmon, folding until it is well mixed. Add enough additional salmon sauce to just coat the salmon. (You will not need all of the sauce mixture. Reserve the remaining sauce, for another use, in an airtight container in the refrigerator.) The fresh herbs should be added to the tartare last. Prepare toast points by toasting bread lightly, removing crusts, and cutting each slice into 4 triangles, or points.

Place a ring mold of the desired portion size onto the plate. Fill the mold to capacity, pat down with the base of a spoon, then gently remove the mold. You should have a perfectly round disk of tartare to wrap with the smoked salmon.

Wrap one slice of smoked salmon around the outside of the tartare, and top the presentation with a dollop of caviar, shaped like a tiny quenelle. Serve the tartare with an ounce or so of pea shoots and toast points, four points per person.

SERVES 6 AS AN APPETIZER

Fiery Shrimp

DAN RUSSO, VIRGIL'S REAL BBQ, NYC

 This is a sautéed shrimp dish, served with white rice.

BUTTER

¼ teaspoon cayenne pepper

¼ teaspoon black pepper, ground fine

⅛ teaspoon red pepper flakes

⅛ teaspoon thyme

⅛ teaspoon fresh rosemary

⅛ teaspoon oregano

    Pinch salt

½ pound (2 sticks) butter

SHRIMP

1 pound prawn-size shrimp (20–25 per pound)

BROTH

½ teaspoon garlic, minced

1 teaspoon olive oil

1 quart shrimp stock

1 pint Anchor Steam Beer

1 teaspoon Worcestershire sauce

    Parsley for garnish

First, prepare the butter. Combine the cayenne pepper, black pepper, red pepper flakes, thyme, rosemary, oregano, and salt with the butter. Knead into firm butter and roll into a cylinder about 2 inches in diameter. Wrap in plastic wrap and refrigerate.

Shell and de-vein the shrimp. Set aside until later in the preparation.
In a soup pot, sauté the garlic in a small amount of olive oil. When almost brown, add the shrimp stock, beer, and Worcestershire sauce. Bring to a boil and simmer for 1 hour. Strain the broth into a bowl and reserve for later in the recipe.
In a hot skillet, toss the shrimp with two tablespoons of the prepared butter. Remove the shrimp when just opaque white and pink. Do not overcook. Deglaze the pan with 2 cups of shrimp broth and reduce by one half.

Make a bed of about ½ cup of white rice on an oval plate. Arrange 6–8 shrimp on the rice. Spoon a few tablespoons of reduced sauce over the shrimp. Dress with a sprinkle of parsley.

SERVES 6 AS AN APPETIZER

Ale-Battered Shrimp and Onion Rings

CHEF BILL DOWNEY, EDWARD MORANS, NYC

Chef Downey notes that, "At Edward Moran Bar and Grill we serve the dish as follows. Place a small stem glass of ale (same as used in the batter) on a beverage napkin placed in the middle of a 9-inch plate. Arrange 6 onion rings and 6 shrimp around the glass of beer."

3	whole large eggs
2	cups Pete's Wicked Ale or Bass Ale
3	cups all-purpose flour
1	tablespoon kosher salt
1	teaspoon white pepper
3	large Spanish onions
12	pieces 16/20 Tiger shrimp
1	quart soy oil

GARNISH

2	sprigs fresh parsley, chopped
1	sprig fresh thyme, chopped

Beat eggs in a large bowl. Add the beer slowly, then whisk in the flour. Season with salt and pepper. Peel and slice onions approximately ½-inch thick and pop out large rings. Save small pieces for stock. Peel and de-vein shrimp leaving no shell. Dip onion and shrimp into batter mixture, one piece at a time, shaking off excess batter, and float in the hot oil for 2 minutes, or until golden brown. Drain on a paper towel and sprinkle with garnish.

SERVES 4

Big River Rocket Red Chicken

CHEF RICHARD HAMILTON, BIG RIVER GRILLE & BREWING WORKS, CHATTANOOGA, TN

2 tablespoons unsalted butter, room temperature

2 tablespoons vegetable oil

4 chicken breasts, flattened

2 tablespoons flour (salted and peppered to taste)

3 cups shiitake mushrooms, julienne

1 cup scallions

1 cup **Big River Rocket Red Reduction** (recipe follows)

$1/2$ cup heavy cream

   Salt and pepper to taste

$1/2$ teaspoon molasses (optional)

$1/2$ teaspoon balsamic vinegar (optional)

Heat butter and oil in skillet. Dredge chicken breasts in flour mixture. Sauté until golden brown on both sides. Remove from skillet. Sauté shiitake mushrooms and scallions, and cook until mushrooms give up moisture and turn slightly brown. Add **Big River Rocket Red Reduction** and reduce by one half. Finish with cream, salt, and pepper. Adjust seasonings. (If too bitter, add $1/2$ teaspoon each of molasses and balsamic vinegar.) Pour sauce into bowl.

Place chicken breast on dinner plate. Dress with sauce and mushrooms. Place starch (rice or potatoes) on one side of chicken. Place fresh, cooked vegetables (sautéed carrot julienne or sautéed green beans) on other side.

SERVES 4

Big River Rocket Red Reduction

CHEF RICHARD HAMILTON, BIG RIVER GRILLE & BREWING WORKS, CHATTANOOGA, TN

CHICKEN AND BEER STOCK

½	cup carrots, diced
½	cup onions, diced
¼	cup celery, diced
1	tablespoon olive oil
1½	pounds chicken wings
1	bay leaf
1½	quart water
1	pint amber beer
	Pinch Kosher salt
	Pinch freshly ground black pepper

½	cup carrots, diced
½	cup onion, diced
¼	cup celery, diced
1	bottle Rocket Red Ale/amber beer
1½	cups of chicken and beer stock
1	teaspoon apple cider vinegar
1	teaspoon molasses
	Pinch Kosher salt
	Pinch ground black pepper

In a large pot, sauté the vegetables in oil until soft. Add chicken and brown. Toss bay leaf on top of vegetables and chicken and add water and beer, salt and pepper to taste. Simmer for 2 hours or until bones have released almost all meat. Cool and refrigerate. Finished product will gelatinize.

Sauté vegetables until soft. Remove from pan. Deglaze with beer and reduce by one half. Add stock and reduce by one half. Add vinegar and molasses. Salt and pepper to taste.

SERVES 4 (AS PART OF BIG RIVER ROCKET RED CHICKEN)

Braised Chicken in Hefe-Weizen Ale

JOHN GILLIAM,
OZARK BREWING COMPANY, FAYETTEVILLE, AR

1-2¼ pound whole chicken

4   cloves fresh garlic

2   tablespoons salt

2   tablespoons black pepper

1   medium yellow onion
     Twine

1   quart hefe–weizen

2   sprigs fresh rosemary

2   pounds new potatoes

1   pound julienne carrots

1   pound acorn squash

Preheat the oven to 450°F. Wash the inside of the chicken under cold water. Pat chicken dry and season the cavity with the garlic, salt, and pepper. Slice the onion, place in the cavity, and tie off with the twine. Place in a preheated 450°F degree oven for 15 minutes, then reduce the heat to 325°F. Add the weizen, rosemary, potatoes, carrots, and squash. Baste the chicken with the ale every 10 minutes for the next 50 minutes. Remove the chicken and allow to rest for 15 minutes before serving.

You can either serve the vegetables in the broth or strain them out and serve separately.

SERVES 2

Grilled Breast of Chicken Marinated in Boston Ale

DENIS MANNEVILLE, WEBERS, BALTIMORE, MD

1   bunch fresh tarragon, chopped

1   bunch fresh thyme, chopped

1   bunch fresh marjoram, chopped

1   bunch fresh rosemary, chopped

2   12-ounce bottles Boston Ale

4   ounces olive oil

    Salt and pepper to taste

8   6-ounce pieces boneless breast of chicken

2   bunches scallions

6   ounces sun-dried tomatoes

Prepare the marinade one day before needed. Place the chopped tarragon, thyme, marjoram, and rosemary in a bowl. Add the beer, olive oil, salt, and pepper. Place the chicken, in a single layer, in a pan large enough to hold the chicken and marinade. Pour the marinade over the chicken and refrigerate overnight

When ready to cook, place the chicken on a hot grill and mark both sides. Reduce heat and cook until done. Remove to a heated tray. Sauté the scallions and sun-dried tomatoes, just to warm, in half a cup of marinade. Reduce slightly and spoon this sauce over the chicken.

SERVES 4

BREW HOUSE

Grilled Chicken Dijon over Scalloped Potatoes

JOE KUBIK,
JOHN HARVARD'S BREW HOUSE, CAMBRIDGE, MA

 This dish looks best when served garnished with chives and asparagus spears. Serve with either the same ale used in the sauce or a pale ale.

CHICKEN

5   8-ounce chicken breasts, double, boneless, skinless, fully trimmed (no tenderloin)

     Salt and pepper to taste

2   tablespoons olive oil

DIJON MUSTARD

4   tablespoons Dijon mustard, dried

2   tablespoons water

SCALLOPED POTATOES

2½   pounds potatoes, peeled

3   teaspoons salt

1   tablespoon unsalted butter, chopped

1   garlic clove, smashed

1¾   cups heavy cream

NUT BROWN ALE MUSHROOM SAUCE

1   garlic clove, chopped

1   small shallot, chopped

1   tablespoon unsalted butter

9   ounces mushrooms, quartered

6   tablespoons dry white wine

½   pound unsalted butter

¾–1 ounce Nut Brown Ale

     Salt and pepper to taste

¼   cup fresh white bread crumbs

CHICKEN
Sprinkle chicken with salt and pepper. Rub with oil and grill, until just cooked (about two minutes a side for 1-inch thick breasts).

MUSTARD
Mix the mustard and water together.

SCALLOPED POTATOES
Preheat oven to 350°F. Slice the potatoes into ¼-inch thick slices. Toss in salt. Butter an 8 x 8 x 2-inch Pyrex™ dish and rub with butter and smashed garlic clove. Discard the garlic. Lay the potatoes evenly in the dish and cover with 12 ounces heavy cream. Cover with aluminum foil and bake in a 350°F oven for about 45 minutes. Remove the foil, top with the remaining 2 ounces of cream and put back in 450°F oven for about 10 minutes, or until the tops of the potatoes are light brown. Remove from the oven.

NUT BROWN ALE MUSHROOM SAUCE
Sauté garlic and shallots in one tablespoon of butter. Do not allow to color (turn brown). Add the mushrooms. Moisten with the white wine and reduce until almost dry. Remove from the heat and add about 6 ounces of the butter. Shake the pan back and forth to stir the butter into the mushroom and onion mixture. Add the remaining butter, all the while stirring, until all butter is melted. Stir in the beer. Add salt and pepper to taste. Pour the sauce into a gravy boat and set aside in a warm place.

Place a thin coat of mustard on each chicken breast. Dust with fresh white bread crumbs and place under a broiler until golden brown. Remove from the broiler and set aside briefly. Take each plate and place a portion about a cup of potatoes in the center of each plate. Divide the sauce and spoon onto the plate, around the center-piece of scalloped potatoes. Place an individual breast on top of each mound of scalloped potatoes.

SERVES 6

Bistrot Belgique Gourmande

Breast of Duck with Fresh Cherries and Kriek Beer

CHEF DANIELE JOHNSON, BISTROT BELGIQUE GOURMANDE, OCCOQUAN, VA

 Use 2 whole ducks. Freeze the remaining carcass (without the giblets) for use in stock, after removing the breasts from both ducks.

2 whole ducks with breasts removed
4 whole duck breasts
1 tablespoon butter
1 small onion, chopped
1 celery stalk, chopped
 Bouquet garni (2 sprigs parsley, 1 sprig thyme, and 1 bay leaf)
 Salt and pepper to taste
1 cup Kriek beer
2 pounds pitted fresh cherries, or 1 bag frozen

After removing the breasts, chop the duck carcass in 5–6 big large pieces. Melt about 1 tablespoon butter in a heavy pot and sauté the pieces of duck until browned well. Remove as much grease as possible with a baster or large spoon. Add the onion, celery, bouquet garni, and a little salt and pepper. Cover with 4 cups of water and let simmer for 2 hours. Strain the broth, extracting as much juice as possible. Reduce the broth on high heat until 1 ½ cups of liquid remain. Cool the liquid, and degrease. Add the Kriek and the pitted cherries, bring to a simmer, check for salt and pepper and if needed, thicken lightly with a little cornstarch. Keep warm but not cooking. In a large pan, brown the breasts with a little butter, until juices run almost clear when pierced, and add the degreased juices to the sauce; broil the breasts for 4 minutes skin side up. Slice the breasts, place on large, warm serving platter, and pour a little sauce on them.

Serve with shallot/parsley whipped potatoes and steamed asparagus or creamed spinach with the rest of the sauce served in a side boat.

SERVES 4

Duck Confit with Daikon Sprouts and Spicy Tomato Concassée

CHEF WADE SIMPSON, LANTANA GRILLE, PHOENIX, AZ

1	whole duck
2	celery stalks, chopped
1	medium carrot, chopped
1	medium onion, chopped
4	bay leaves
2	tablespoons whole peppercorns
2	cups vegetable oil
4	cups water
1	tablespoon kosher salt
1	rosemary sprig
1	thyme sprig
$^1/_2$	bottle Brasseurs beer

To prepare duck, break down legs and breast, remove the skin from the body. Reserve the breast for another use. Place the skin and all fat from the body cavity, along with the celery, carrot, onion, bay leaves, 1 tablespoon whole peppercorns, 2 cups vegetable oil, and water in a pot. Place on stove at medium-low heat for 2–4 hours to render the fat. Remove the pot from the heat and chill rapidly. When thoroughly chilled, refrigerate. Rub the duck legs with salt, rosemary, thyme and 1 tablespoon of peppercorns. Place legs in a pan, cover with a clean damp towel and refrigerate overnight. The next day remove the towel and pour softened, rendered-fat mixture over duck legs. Place pan on stove over medium-low heat and simmer (do not boil) for about 3 hours or until meat begins to flake from the bone. Add $^1/_2$ bottle Brasseurs Beer. Remove from heat and bring to room temperature. Refrigerate overnight. The next day, remove the duck legs and flake meat off bones and set aside.

TOMATO CONCASSÉE

1   medium tomato, peeled, seeded, and diced

1   red jalapeno, diced, and mixed with tomato

1   head radicchio, julienned

1   head bibb lettuce, julienned

1   head Belgian endive, pulled leaves

1   bunch Daikon sprouts

1   package Enoki mushrooms (found in specially food stores)
    Duck confit

DRESSING

1   cup sherry vinegar

$\frac{1}{2}$ tablespoon whole peppercorns

1   teaspoon whole clove

2   bay leaves

1   cup Brasseurs Beer

$2\frac{1}{2}$ cups hazelnut oil

      Salt and pepper to taste

To prepare the salad, the dressing should be prepared first. Combine sherry vinegar, $\frac{1}{2}$ tablespoon whole peppercorns, clove, and bay leaves in a pan. Simmer until reduced to $\frac{1}{2}$ cup. Strain and add 1 cup Brasseurs Beer. Let cool to room temperature. Whip in hazelnut oil. Season with salt and pepper.

To assemble the salad, mix radicchio and bibb lettuce in a bowl. Toss with 1 cup dressing. On each plate, place Belgian endive leaves at 12, 4, and 8 o'clock positions. Place tossed salad mix in center of the plate and a portion of duck confit on top. Spoon tomato concassée over duck and garnish with daikon sprouts and Enoki mushrooms.

SERVES 6

Baymen's Pie

DON SULLIVAN,
SOUTHHAMPTON PUBLICK HOUSE, SOUTHAMPTON, NY

Excellent accompaniments to this dish are garlic mashed potatoes made with Yukon Gold potatoes, and grilled mixed vegetables brushed with balsamic vinaigrette.

1   large onion, diced

4   large carrots, diced

$1/2$ pound mushrooms, halved

2   tablespoons olive oil

2   pounds stew beef, cubed

$1/4$ cup all-purpose flour

12   oysters, whole, shucked, reserve liquid

1   pint India pale ale

2   cups beef stock

2   tablespoons tomato paste

Parsley, to dress

Pastry, to cover (see "Basic Pastry" on page 116)

Salt and pepper to taste

Sauté the vegetables in the oil until tender, add beef. Cook until rare. Add flour and stir until a light roux is formed. Add the oysters, liquid reserved from oysters, ale, stock, and tomato paste. Cook at low heat, stirring occasionally. Season with salt and pepper, cook for 1 hour. Portion stew into casserole and cover with pastry. Bake until pastry is light brown (about 15 minutes).

If cooked in individual casseroles, serve with side salad and the same beer used to make the dish. If served from a large casserole, family style, ensure that each plate has a slice of pastry and serve with side salad.

SERVES 4

Beef Short Ribs (Braised) with Chipotle Peppers and Wheat Beer

MARK LEWANDOWSKI,
TIED HOUSE CAFE AND BREWERY, MOUNTAIN VIEW, CA

 This dish goes well with any weissbier, from the light, refreshing summer hefe-weizen to the rich dark dunkel-weizen.

4-6 pounds short ribs of beef

2-3 tablespoons bacon drippings

1 cup celery, diced

2 cups onion, diced

1 cup carrots, diced

10 cloves whole garlic, peeled but not chopped

2 or 3 chipotle peppers, diced

2 red bell peppers, charred, peeled and chopped

3/4 cup flour

6 cups rich beef stock

1 cup wheat beer

Salt and pepper to taste

Preheat oven to 250°F. Heat the bacon drippings in a heavy pot over medium-high heat and add the short ribs, browning on all sides. Remove from the pan. Add the celery, onions, carrots, and garlic. Let brown slightly, stirring to bring up the brown bits from the bottom of the pan. Add the chipotle peppers and diced red bell pepper, and sauté for 5 minutes. Sprinkle in the flour and cook until the roux takes on a dark brown color. Slowly add the beef stock. Bring to a boil and then turn the heat down to simmer.

Add the beer and put the ribs back in the pan. Place in the preheated oven for 2-3 hours or until the meat is ready to fall off the bone. If the sauce begins to reduce too much, cover the pan.

To serve, remove the ribs from the pan and keep warm. Remove any fat from the top of the sauce with a large spoon or shallow ladle. Taste the sauce and add salt and pepper to taste. If the sauce is too thin, place over a high heat to reduce to desired thickness. Serve the sauce and vegetables over the short ribs.

SERVES 4-6

Scott and Jamie's 'Texas Lovers' Chili

CHEF SCOTT COHEN, THE STANHOPE, NYC

There is a story here!

16 ounces dried kidney beans, soaked in cold water overnight

6 cups water

3½ teaspoons chili powder

4 ancho chilies, soaked, seeded, and finely diced

1 poblano pepper, seeded and finely diced

2 jalapeños seeded and finely diced

½ tablespoon onion powder

¼ tablespoon garlic powder

1 tablespoon ground cumin

½ teaspoon cracked black pepper

Salt to taste

4 pounds ground beef

1 medium onion, finely diced

2 cloves garlic, minced

1½ pounds canned stewed tomatoes, finely diced

5 ounces tomato paste

2 smoked ham hocks

Wash beans in cold water, drain. Cover in mixing bowl with cold water, about 2 inches over beans, and soak at least 8 hours, or overnight.

Drain the beans and pour into a large kettle. Add 6 cups water, chili powder, and ancho chilies, bring to a boil, and simmer 2 hours. Add poblano pepper, jalapeños, onion powder, garlic powder, cumin, cracked black pepper, and salt to taste (about 1 teaspoon to start).

Cover and simmer over 3 hours. Let mixture chill about 6-8 hours or, overnight.

In a large sauce pot sauté the ground beef until golden brown, add onions and garlic and cook until onions are soft. Remove from stove and drain excess grease. Add beef-onion-garlic mixture to bean mixture. Add stewed tomatoes, tomato paste, and smoked ham hocks. Bring to a boil and simmer for 2 hours. Adjust seasoning with additional salt or pepper.

Serve in bowls accompanied by taco chips. Garnishes can include diced cheddar or Monterey Jack cheese, chopped red onion, chopped cilantro, and sour cream.

SERVES 6

Guinness-Sauced Lamb Sausage on Tomato Fettuccine

JOHN ZENGER, RIVER PLACE HOTEL, PORTLAND, OR

RiverPlace Hotel

1	pound lightly spiced lamb sausage, sliced or diced
2	tablespoons shallots, minced
1	tablespoon garlic, minced
1/2	pound sliced button mushrooms
3/4	cup Guinness
2 1/2	cups heavy cream
1/2	log Montrachet goat cheese
1	pound fresh tomato fettuccine
6–7	fresh mint leaves, chopped

Brown the sausage over medium to medium-low heat, until fully cooked. Remove all but a teaspoon of the fat, and add the shallots, garlic, and mushrooms. Sweat until they are wilted but not colored. Remove the shallots, garlic, and mushrooms and set aside with the browned sausage. Deglaze the pan with the Guinness and reduce to almost a syrup. Return the sausage, shallots, garlic, and mushrooms to the pan and add the heavy cream. Crumble the cheese into the cream. Stir until melted. (The cheese will thicken the sauce without having to do a second reduction.) Bring a pot of water to a boil and cook fettuccine. Serve the sauce over fettuccine and sprinkle with freshly chopped mint leaves.

SERVES 4

GRANITE BREWERY

Braised Lamb Shanks in Pale Ale

CLARK NICKERSON,
GRANITE BREWERY, TORONTO, ONTARIO, CANADA

6	lamb shanks
14	ounces plum tomatoes
½	pint pale ale
1	carrot, chopped into large pieces
1	stalk celery, chopped into large pieces
1	clove garlic, chopped into small pieces
½	teaspoon dried thyme
½	teaspoon dried rosemary
1	tablespoon tomato paste
	Salt and pepper to taste

Preheat oven to 375°F. Brown the lamb shanks, on all sides, in a large pan. Combine all other ingredients in a 2-quart sauce pan. Bring to a boil. Place lamb shanks in a roasting pan and cover with liquid. Roast (covered) in preheated oven for approximately 3 hours, turning shanks every half hour to ensure even cooking.

Serve over white rice or mashed potatoes and fresh vegetables.

SERVES 6

Pizza Kitchen & Brewery

Osso Buco á la Boscos

ANDY FINESTONE, BOSCOS, GERMANTOWN, TN

½   cup olive oil

¼   cup butter

1   cup flour
    Salt and pepper to taste

6   lamb shanks (cut in 2-inch sections)

1½ cups stone beer

2   medium carrots, chopped

3   stalks celery

2   medium onions, chopped

3   tablespoons garlic, chopped

1   quart chicken stock

½   cup orange juice concentrate

Preheat the oven to 300°F. Heat the oil and butter in a skillet. Next, flour lamb and season with salt and pepper. Brown in a pan and deglaze with the stone beer. Remove the lamb and reserve the sauce. Add carrots, celery, onion, and garlic to a braising pan, place the lamb on top of the vegetables, and add chicken stock, orange juice, and sauce from deglazing sauce. Bake in a 300°F oven for 1 hour, or until meat pulls away from the bone. Serve with rice or buttered noodles and fresh steamed vegetables.

SERVES 6

Grilled Pork Chops
with a Yucatan Orange-Chile Recado

(SERVED WITH A POTATO CELERY ROOT PANCAKE)

CHEF JOSEPH ELORRIAGA, MIRACLE GRILL, NYC

This is a unique German/Mexican combination. A recado is a Mexican preparation of toasted spices and chilies ground into a paste and moistened with Seville orange juice.

RECADO

2   ancho chili pods, seeded

2   tablespoons cumin seed

2   teaspoons allspice berries

3   chipotle peppers, including adobo

5   garlic cloves

1   bunch cilantro

3/4   cup orange juice

1/4   cup lime juice

2   tablespoons Tabasco sauce

2   teaspoons kosher salt

1/4   cup virgin olive oil

8   center-cut pork chops, 3/4-inch thick
    Vegetable oil
    Kosher salt and pepper

Prepare the recado in advance: Place the ancho chili pods, cumin seed, and allspice berries in a medium-hot skillet and toss lightly until lightly toasted and fragrant; then grind the mixture in a spice mill. Place all of the recado ingredients, except the olive oil, in a food processor and blend until a smooth paste is formed. Then slowly blend in the olive oil. Set aside. Prepare the pancake mixture (recipe follows). Brush the pork lightly with vegetable oil and season with salt and pepper. Place the chops on a hot grill and cook on both sides until desired doneness (medium is recommended). Brush the recado on the chops.

Serve the pork chop with the hot pancakes and a chilled Mexican-style lager, such as Dos Equis. Sip the beer between bites of the food. Continue until a level of satisfaction has been achieved.

SERVES 4

Potato Celery Root Pancake

CHEF JOSEPH ELORRIAGA, MIRACLE GRILL, NYC

1½ cups grated potatoes

½ grated celery root

3 eggs

1½ tablespoons all-purpose flour

1¼ teaspoons salt

1 tablespoon grated onion
Bacon fat or vegetable oil for frying

Place the grated potatoes and celery root in a cloth and squeeze out as much liquid as possible. Combine the vegetables with the eggs, flour, salt, and onion. Heat the bacon fat or oil in a large skillet until just smoking. Spoon 3 x ¼-inch patties into skillet and cook until golden brown and crispy. Turn and continue cooking until the pancake is cooked through.

SERVES 4

Pan Roasted Pork Tenderloin

MICKY DOWD, ALDEN COUNTRY INN, LYME, NH

1   tablespoon salt
1   tablespoon cracked black pepper
1   tablespoon whole rosemary
2   8-ounce tenderloins of pork
2   tablespoons unsalted butter
1   medium white onion, chopped
½   cup shallots, chopped
1   garlic clove, chopped
1   cup chicken/beer stock (see beef stock recipe on page 115)
1   cup mango chutney (Major Grey)

Mix salt, cracked black pepper, and rosemary on a dish and roll the pork tenderloins in the mixture until coated. Place tenderloins in a hot pan with butter and sauté over medium heat until browned, rolling the meat to brown on ALL sides. Set aside. Preheat oven to 350°F. In a sauce pan over medium heat combine onions, shallots, and garlic in a tablespoon of butter and sauté until the onion is translucent. Add chicken stock and chutney and heat. Set aside. Finish pork in a 350°F oven, in the same pan used for browning, for 15 minutes (should be served just pink).

Place sauce on plate and fan pieces of pork over it. Garnish with rice and choice of sautéed or steamed vegetables. I find that this dish goes very well with a beer such as Catamount Amber.

SERVES 2

Three Sausages with Caramelized Onions and Apples

BRICKTOWN BREWERY
R E S T A U R A N T

DAVID MILLIGAN,
BRICKTOWN BREWERY, OKLAHOMA CITY, OK

Chef Milligan suggests, "Use three different types of sausage. Fresh hand-made sausages are best if you have them. We use bratwurst, andouille, and chicken/apple sausage."

12	sausages (2–3 ounces each)
1/4	pound butter
2	large yellow onions, julienned
3	Granny Smith apples, peeled, cored, and sliced
1/4	cup brown sugar
1/4	cup balsamic vinegar
1/2	cup brown ale

Boil the sausages until cooked through. Set aside and keep warm. Melt butter in a large skillet and add the onions. When onions are clear, add apples and cook for 5 minutes. Add the brown sugar, balsamic vinegar, and ale. Cook until the liquid is reduced to the consistency of syrup. Grill sausages until browned and serve over onions and apples.

SERVES 4

Red Beans and Rice with Andouille Sausage

CHEF JACK SEDIVY,
SILO MICROBREWERY, LOUISVILLE, KY

2   gallons dried red beans, soaked overnight in cold water

3   gallons of water, but you have to keep adding water as the beans cook

    Salt to taste

6   cups onion, diced

6   cups green bell pepper, diced

7   cups celery, diced

1½ cups seasoning mix (use Paul Prudhomme or any other popular Louisiana seasoning)

3   pounds andouille sausage, diced

Prepare the beans by soaking overnight. Cook the beans in water with salt to taste until firm, but not mushy. Sauté the "trinity" (onion, pepper, and celery) until tender, add the seasoning mixture, and then the sausage. Add the beans, then water, and simmer for 2–4 hours. Adjust the seasoning with salt and pepper, and serve over rice.

SERVES 12

Grilled New York Strip Steak with Samuel Adams Triple Bock Onion Confit and Madagascar Sauce

DENIS MANNEVILLE, WEBERS, BALTIMORE, MD

MARINADE

- ½ cup olive oil
- 4 cloves garlic, crushed
- 4 sprigs rosemary
- ½ bunch fresh oregano, chopped
- ½ bunch fresh thyme, chopped
  Freshly ground pepper and sea salt to taste
- 4 12-ounce New York strip steaks
- ¼ cup whole black peppercorns

MADAGASGAR SAUCE

- 2 tablespoons butter
- ¼ cup finely chopped shallots
- ¼ cup Cognac
- ½ cup veal stock
- ¼ cup whole 4-color peppercorns

TRIPLE BOCK ONION CONFIT

- 4 small yellow onions, chopped
- 2 tablespoons olive oil
- 1 bottle Samuel Adams Triple Bock
  Salt and pepper to taste

Place olive oil, crushed garlic, rosemary, oregano, and thyme, salt and pepper in a pan. Marinate the steaks in this mixture for 12 hours. Remove the steaks and press into crushed peppercorns until covered. Grill until medium rare.

Prepare the Madagascar sauce by placing 1 ounce of butter in saucepan to melt. Add the shallots and cook until soft. Add the Cognac and reduce. Add the veal stock and reduce. Add the peppercorns and remove from heat.

Prepare the onion confit by sautéing the onions in the olive oil. Add the Triple Bock and simmer until the onions are soft. Add salt and pepper to taste.

Pour about 1 tablespoon of sauce on a plate. Place the steak on the sauce and cover the steak with the onion confit.

SERVES 4

Venison Sausage

CHEF DAVID PAGE, HOME, NYC

 This trio is very autumnal and hearty

1	pound ground venison shoulder
1½	pounds ground pork
¼	teaspoon crushed juniper berries
½	teaspoon lemon zest
½	teaspoon orange zest
1	teaspoon garlic, minced
1	teaspoon minced fresh marjoram
1	teaspoon Kosher salt
½	teaspoon ground black pepper
3	tablespoons olive oil

Combine all the ingredients and form into 6 patties. Sauté in a hot pan with the olive oil for 3 minutes on each side. Serve with **Boston Brown Bread** and **Baked Cranberry Beans.**

SERVES 4

·HOME· RESTAURANT

·HOME·

RESTAURANT

Boston Brown Bread

CHEF DAVID PAGE, HOME, NYC

 This is probably the easiest recipe in this book, but it takes the longest time—be prepared!

½	cup rye flour
½	cup whole wheat flour
½	cup cornmeal
¾	teaspoon baking soda
¾	teaspoon salt
1	cup buttermilk
½	cup raisins

In a large mixing bowl fold together all the ingredients. The dough can then be steamed in a covered coffee can placed in a simmering water bath for 3½ hours. (Keep an eye on the water bath–it evaporates!) When a finger pressed to surface does not leave an imprint, the bread is done–try to stay to three and a half-hour time frame. It is hard to overcook this bread.

SERVES 4

Baked Cranberry Beans

CHEF DAVID PAGE, HOME, NYC

This is a two-part recipe. First is the bean prep, followed by the actual baking process.

1   carrot, roughly chopped

1   stalk celery, chopped

1   bay leaf

8   black peppercorns

1   sprig thyme

8   cups salted water

3   cups cranberry beans, soaked overnight

3   tablespoons molasses

1   cup minced bacon

1½ cups diced onions

½   cup diced celery

1½ cup diced green pepper

1   minced jalapeño pepper

1   cup brown or chicken stock

1   cup water

2   tablespoons equal parts minced thyme/rosemary/parsley

2   bay leaves

2   tablespoons tomato paste

    Salt and pepper to taste

Make a sachet with the carrot, celery, bay leaf, peppercorns, and thyme, and simmer in salted water with the beans and molasses for 1–2 hours, or until the beans are tender. Then, in a heavy, oven-proof pot, render the fat from the bacon, add the onion, celery, green pepper, and jalapeño. Sweat the mixture until translucent. Add the cooked beans and remaining ingredients. Bring to a boil and bake in a 350°F oven for 1½ hours, or until you remember them. (Don't worry–they will smell delicious!)

SERVES 4-6

Roasted Venison Tenderloin in a Cherry-Herb Crust, Glazed with Samuel Adams Cherry Wheat Beer

CHEF-OWNER LUCIE P. COSTA,
NORTH PLANK ROAD TAVERN, NEWBURGH, NY

The Historic
North Plank Road
Tavern
1851

This dish, with Wilted Arugula and Sautéed Mixed Mushrooms and Herb Texmati Rice, forms a fine Autumn Menu. Serve with a rich, amber ale that can stand up to the rich flavors of the venison, sauce and the bitter flavors of the arugula side dish.

8   4-ounce medallions of venison tenderloin
Salt and pepper to taste
1   cup clarified butter

CHERRY-HERB CRUST

1   cup tart dried cherries, chopped
1   cup garlic, minced
1   cup shallot, minced
1/2 cup fresh chives, chopped
1/2 cup fresh parsley, chopped
1/2 cup fresh rosemary, chopped
1/2 cup fresh thyme, chopped
1   cup brown stock (if not available, substitute canned beef consommé)
Salt and pepper to taste

GLAZE

1   bottle of cherry wheat beer
Roux (if not available, substitute arrowroot or cornstarch)
Salt and pepper to taste

Season the meat with salt and pepper. In a sauté pan, over high heat, sear the meat in the butter on all sides. Remove the meat from the pan and deglaze the pan with cherry wheat beer, reserving the liquid for the sauce. Cover the meat and set aside. Preheat oven to 375°F.

Mix all ingredients for the cherry-herb crust except stock in a bowl. Place mixture on a clean, flat surface and roll the venison tenderloin in it until the tenderloin is completely covered. Place the venison in a roasting pan. Add brown stock, cover and cook in a 375°F oven until the meat reaches 135°F (rare). Add salt and pepper to taste. Set aside and let rest a few minutes before slicing.

Strain the liquid from the roasting pan. Combine liquid from sauté pan with the liquid from the roasting pan. Add cherry wheat beer and reduce by 1/3. Add the roux to thicken and reduce again until the sauce has the consistency of chocolate sauce. Season with salt and pepper. Keep warm until serving.

SERVES 4

The Historic
North Plank Road
Tavern
1851

(Wilted) Arugula and Sautéed Mixed Mushrooms

**CHEF-OWNER LUCIE P. COSTA,
NORTH PLANK ROAD TAVERN, NEWBURGH, NY**

4   cups mixed mushrooms (portobello, shiitake, buttons and chanterelle), quartered

2   tablespoons clarified butter

1   tablespoon herbes de Provence (mixture of marjoram, thyme, rosemary, fennel seed, and parsley)

White wine

Salt and pepper to taste

3   tablespoons minced garlic

2   cups arugula, cleaned, stemmed, cut, chiffonnade

Sauté mushrooms in a sauté pan with the butter, the herbes de Provence, a splash of white wine, and the salt and pepper. Stir in garlic, add arugula. Set aside for service.

SERVES 4

Herb Texmati Rice

The Historic North Plank Road Tavern 1881

CHEF-OWNER LUCIE P. COSTA,
NORTH PLANK ROAD TAVERN, NEWBURGH, NY

2   cups white Texmati rice

4   cups chicken broth

2   tablespoons fresh parsley, chopped

     Salt and pepper to taste

½   cup tart dried cherries (rehydrated in Port wine), chopped

1   cup garlic cloves, roasted until golden brown in 350°F oven

1   cup roasted pecans

1   tablespoon fresh thyme, chopped

Cook rice in chicken broth. Add the parsley, salt and pepper. Combine cherries, garlic, pecan, and thyme. Press rice mixture inside a 2-inch ring or put into a small ramekin and unmold for service.

In the center of the plate, place rice timbale, fan pieces of venison around it with sautéed mushrooms, add cherry wheat beer sauce alongside and over meat, and serve.

SERVES 4

Mesclun Greens Salad with Cherry Wheat Vinaigrette

CHEF DENIS MANNEVILLE,
WEBERS, BALTIMORE, MD

 A basic salad that is quite complex in its simplicity. With the aroma of cherry and the hint of sour cherry in the flavor, it is essential that the freshest herbs possible be used.

VINAIGRETTE

1   tablespoon dry mustard
2   tablespoons apple cider vinegar
5   sprigs of chopped fresh thyme
5   sprigs of chopped fresh basil
6   tablespoons virgin olive oil
1/2 cup cherry wheat beer
     Salt and pepper to taste

1   cup mesclun greens
1/2 cup artichoke hearts (glass jars of artichoke hearts can be found in specialty food shops)
1/4 cup freshly toasted pecans
1/2 cup feta cheese

In a large bowl, mix the dry mustard and apple cider vinegar. Add the thyme and basil, half the oil, and the beer. Whisk well. Add the rest of the oil and mix well. Add the greens to the dressing and toss lightly covering each leaf.

Decorate each plate with the artichoke hearts, portion the dressed greens to each plate. Sprinkle the pecans on top. The feta cheese is sprinkled around the edge of the plate just at the edge of the lettuce.

SERVES 4

Ozark Brewing Co.
Barbecue Sauce with IPA

JOHN GILLIAM,
OZARK BREWING COMPANY, FAYETTEVILLE AR

 This is restaurant quantity—reduce by one half for a big barbecue or half again for home use.

64	ounces India pale ale
2	large yellow onions, puréed
2	green bell peppers, puréed
3	#10 cans chili sauce
32	ounces red wine vinegar
1/2	gallon soy sauce
4	pounds brown sugar
2	tablespoons white pepper
2	tablespoons black pepper
2	tablespoons cayenne pepper
2	tablespoons crushed red pepper

Reduce the IPA by half. When it is almost there, add the onions and the bell peppers. Add all the other ingredients and bring to a simmer. Cook at a simmer for 1 hour.

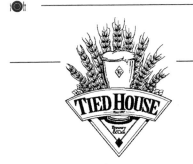

Beer Mustard Chicken Marinade

MARK LEWANDOWSKI,
TIED HOUSE CAFE AND BREWERY, MOUNTAIN VIEW, CA

This is a restaurant-sized recipe. It is best used for a big barbecue. Cut recipe in half for home use.

¼ cup dry mustard
½ cup Dijon mustard
2 tablespoons garlic powder
1 tablespoon chopped fresh thyme
1 tablespoon chopped fresh rosemary
2 tablespoons kosher salt
1 tablespoon ground black peppercorns
½ cup molasses
1 quart olive oil
1 quart dark beer

Place all ingredients except the oil and beer in the bowl of a mixer with a wire whip. Mix until well blended. With the mixer still running on high speed, slowly add the olive oil to form a thick dressing. Then, with the mixer still running, slowly add the beer. Use caution, being careful not to allow the dressing to separate.

HOW TO USE

Place the chicken breasts in a bowl and add just enough marinade to cover. Be sure to mix the chicken with the marinade to ensure that each piece is well covered. Marinate for at least 2 days, but no more that 4 days.

Remove the chicken from the marinade and grill over a hot fire until done (about 2–3 minutes on each side). Garnish with fresh rosemary sprigs.

Present this dish with garlic mashed potatoes made with Yukon Gold potatoes, and grilled mixed vegetables brushed with balsamic vinaigrette.

QUANTITY: 1/2 GALLON

Swans Arctic Ale Cream Sauce

JOHN GALLICHAN, SWANS BREWPUB/BUCKERFIELD'S
BREWERY, VICTORIA, B.C., CANADA

1	tablespoon garlic, chopped
1	tablespoon ginger, grated
1/4	cup chopped white onion
2	tablespoons butter
2	tablespoons olive oil
4	tablespoons flour
1/2	cup light cream
1	cup Arctic Ale (a light, low-alcohol ale)
1	teaspoon lemon zest
1	teaspoon thyme
1	teaspoon parsley
1/2	cup lemon juice
1/2	cup rich chicken stock
1	bay leaf
	Salt and pepper to taste

Sauté the garlic, ginger and onion in the butter and olive oil until the onion is wilted. Add the flour and cook lightly (do not brown). Combine the cream and ale in a bowl. Slowly whisk the cream and ale into the sauté. Whisk until smooth. Add the lemon zest, thyme, and parsley. Combine the lemon juice and stock in a bowl.
Whisk the lemon juice/stock into the sauce. Add the bay leaf and simmer 2–3 minutes. (Add more beer if the sauce gets too thick.) When sauce coats a spoon, remove from heat and salt and pepper to taste.
To adapt this sauce to specific dishes, you may substitute any number of herbs for the thyme: dill for fish, tarragon for chicken, rosemary for pork, etc

SERVES 6

Beer Glazed Potatoes

BILL KUNZ, GROWLER'S PUB, ST. LOUIS, MO

This is a good dish to use up any leftover cooked potatoes you may have. You can prepare this dish and save in the refrigerator until needed. Simply remove the desired amount and follow the presentation directions below.

¼   cup margarine

2   tablespoons olive oil

2   pounds baked potatoes, firm, sliced

¼   cup onions, finely chopped

½   cup amber beer

¼   cup green bell pepper, finely chopped

1   teaspoon thyme

1   teaspoon rosemary

½   teaspoon Kosher salt

½   teaspoon ground black pepper

Heat margarine and olive oil over medium heat until hot. Add potatoes and onions and sauté for 10 minutes. Add beer, green pepper, and herbs, simmer on high heat until beer is reduced by ¾ of the original amount. Add salt and pepper and cook for 10 minutes on low heat, stirring occasionally. For presentation, place a serving in a small skillet and brown thoroughly. Garnish with parsley.

SERVES 4

Harbor Bay Gourmet French Potato Salad

JEFF SCHAGRIN, HARBOR BAY GOURMET, STUART, FL

5 pounds new red potatoes (the smaller the better)

1 pound smoked lean bacon

1 package ranch dressing (made to package instructions)

Bunch scallions, chopped fine

2 cups mayonnaise

1 tablespoon Dijon mustard

Preheat oven to 350°F. Bake the potatoes in a pan in the oven for about 30 minutes. With 10 minutes left in the baking time, place the bacon, on a rack, in the oven and bake until crisp. When potatoes are cooked (a fork will insert easily into one of the potatoes), remove from the oven and put aside to cool. When the bacon is crisp, remove from the oven, crumble, and reserve the drippings.

In a bowl, combine the ranch dressing, scallions, mayonnaise, and mustard. Put aside.

Let the potatoes and bacon cool just to room temperature. If the ingredients are too hot, the dressing will separate. If the ingredients are too cold, they will not absorb the flavors.

Cut the potatoes into thirds or fourths and, as you cut them up, toss them in the dressing mixture. Pour about ¼ cup of the bacon drippings over the potatoes, sprinkle on the bacon, and give a final mix to coat all the potatoes.

This salad is a good accompaniment to hot and cold sandwiches, traditional boiled or steamed "shore dinners," or with a plate of assorted cold meats and pickles. The best beer to serve with this side dish is a rich ale that has enough hops to freshen the palate.

QUANTITY: 5 POUNDS

Sushi Rice

THE INN AT
MAPLEWOOD FARM

LAURA SIMOES,
THE INN AT MAPLEWOOD FARM, HILLSBOROUGH, VT

3⅓ cups short-grain rice

4 cups water

VINEGAR MIXTURE

5 tablespoons plus 1 teaspoon rice vinegar

5 tablespoons sugar

4 teaspoons salt

Wash the rice until the water runs clear. Drain in a colander for 1 hour. Place the drained rice in a rice cooker or in a pot with a close-fitting lid and add water. Cover and bring to a boil over a medium heat. Cover tightly and boil for 2 minutes. Reduce heat to medium and boil for another 5 minutes. Over low heat, cook for 15 minutes or until all the water has been absorbed.

While the rice is cooking, combine the vinegar mixture in an enamel pot and heat slowly until the sugar has dissolved, stirring constantly. Take off heat, and place the pot over ice cubes to cool it quickly. Empty the rice into a nonmetallic tub and spread it out evenly with a flat wooden spoon. Take off the lid, spread a clean kitchen towel over the top of the pot, replace the lid, and let stand for 10–15 minutes to absorb extra moisture.

Run the spoon through the rice in right to left slicing motions to separate the grains. As you do this, slowly add the vinegar mixture. You may not use all of the liquid. Avoid adding too much liquid as this will make your rice mushy.

At the same time that you are mixing the rice, fan the rice to cool it. The fanning and mixing takes about 10 minutes. Do not refrigerate the rice but keep it cool and covered with a clean towel. It will only last one day.

From *The Book of Sushi* by Kinjiro Omae and Yazuru Tachibana.

THE INN AT
MAPLEWOOD FARM

Butter Crust Beer Bread

CHEF LAURA SIMOES,
THE INN AT MAPLEWOOD FARM, HILLSBOROUGH, NH

 Adapted from Mary Emmerling's *American Country Cooking* (Clarkson N. Potter, 1987)

2 cups bread flour

3 tablespoons sugar

1 12-ounce bottle of Catamount American Wheat

nonstick spray

4 tablespoons melted butter

Preheat the oven to 350°F. Mix the flour and sugar in a medium-sized bowl. Slowly add the Catamount American Wheat while stirring. The batter will be sticky. Prepare 2 mini-loaf baking pans by coating with nonstick spray. Divide batter between pans. Bake for 20 minutes. remove from oven and pour half of the melted butter over each loaf. Return the pans to the oven for an additional 20 minutes or until light brown in color. Cool in the pans on wire racks.

Note: If you are substituting for the Catamount American Wheat you must use a beer that is hefe-weissen (has yeast suspended in the beer), or is "bottle conditioned," that is, has active yeast packed to the bottom of the bottle. Many craft beers are bottle conditioned.

MAKES 2 LOAVES

Russian Black Bread

DELMAR CRIM, EMPIRE BREWING, SYRACUSE, NY

4	ounces solid semi-sweet chocolate
3	cups brewed coffee, hot
2	ounces fresh yeast
9	cups whole wheat flour
6	cups rye flour
3	cups bran
8	ounces butter
2	tablespoons caraway seeds
1	tablespoon chopped fennel
4	tablespoons salt
8	ounces minced raw onions
8	ounces molasses
3	cups stout or porter

Add the chocolate to the coffee and let set until warm and the chocolate is melted. Add the fresh yeast and let set for 5 minutes. Add the rest of the ingredients and mix or knead for 8 minutes using flour to dust as needed. Put in an oiled bowl and let rise for 1 hour in a warm place until doubled in size. Preheat oven to 325°F. Grease 4 loaf pans. Punch down, shape, and divide into four balls. Reshape into ball shapes. Put into greased pans and let rise until doubled in size. Bake in a 325°F oven for 45 minutes.

MAKES 4 MEDIUM LOAVES

Stone Beer Bread

ANDY FINESTONE, BOSCOS, GERMANTOWN, TN

2 packets of baking yeast
1 cup warm water
1 cup stone beer (or porter)
2 tablespoons malt extract (see note)
6 ounces melted margarine
4 ounces molasses
5 cups bread flour
   Nonstick spray or a paper towel
   smeared with margarine
1 tablespoon salt
¼ cup butter

Stir the yeast into a cup of warm water. (Hot water from the tap will kill the yeast.) Let the water and yeast sit at room temperature for 15 minutes.

When the yeast has a nice layer of foam on top, it is ready. In a large bowl, mix the beer, malt extract, melted margarine, and molasses. Add the yeast and stir to mix. Add two cups of flour and mix to form a stiff dough. Add another cup of flour and mix to a sticky ball. Add additional flour until the dough can be handled.

Spread about a cup of flour over a 4-square-foot area. Place the ball of dough in the front part of this work area, the area nearest you. Using the heels of your hands push the ball of dough out over the flour that covers the work area, bringing your right heel slightly to the top of the area and letting your left heel fall slightly to the bottom of the area. Bring the far edge of the now slightly flattened ball of dough up from the work surface and fold it over the area where your hands have been. This folding of the dough (called *kneading*) that has been pressed into the flour give the bread an even texture.

Knead the dough until the layers of flour and dough begin to tear slightly, making rips in the surface of the dough. When this happens, form the dough into a ball and place it in a bowl in a warm place. It should rise and double in size. This should take and hour or so. When this has happened, you should use your fist and punch into the center of the dough and fold the edges into the center. Roll the ball of dough over and let rise again. This time you punch the dough down and cut the dough in half with a sharp knife. Preheat the oven to 375°F.

Use nonstick spray or a paper towel smeared with margarine to coat the inside of two loaf pans. Form the dough into shapes that will fit into the bottom of the pans. Place in the preheated oven and bake for a half hour. Keep a close eye on the bread and take it out as soon as the top is light brown. Use a finger and make an indentation on the top of each loaf. When the surface springs back it should be done.

Slip the loaf out of the pan and thump the bottom of the loaf with your finger. If there is a hollow sound the bread is ready. If not, bake for an additional ten minutes and test again.

Note: Malt extract can be purchased from home-brew supply shops. It comes in an aluminum can weighing about 3.3 pounds. Make sure you get unhopped extract. Use the leftover extract as you would corn syrup or molasses. A spoonful is great on hot oatmeal.

MAKES 2 LOAVES

Beer Yeast Rolls

CHEF RICHARD HAMILTON, BIG RIVER GRILLE & BREWING WORKS, CHATTANOOGA, TN

2   sticks (½ pound.) margarine
¾   cups water
1½   cups milk
¾   cups beer
½   cup sugar
4   cups all-purpose flour
2   packages yeast
3   eggs
2   teaspoons honey

Melt margarine in a saucepan. Stir in water, milk, and beer. Heat until liquid is warm, remove from heat. In a bowl, sift sugar, flour, and yeast and mix thoroughly. Combine eggs and honey in a bowl and beat lightly with a whisk. Add egg/honey mixture to the dry ingredients and mix thoroughly. Slowly add liquids to the batter. Beat with wire whisk until consistency is slightly lumpy. Refrigerate for 2 hours. Preheat oven to 400°F. Grease 12-muffin pan. Spoon batter into greased muffin pans and bake for 15 minutes. Rolls will be done when toothpick stuck in the middle comes out clean. Remove from oven and let sit until warm. Brush with melted margarine and serve.

MAKES 12 MEDIUM ROLLS/MUFFINS

Fruit Tempura with St. Landelin Basil Sorbet

CHEF WADE SIMPSON, LANTANA GRILLE, PHOENIX, AZ

SORBET

1/2	cup sugar
1	cup water
1	cup dry white wine
12	basil leaves
1	bottle St. Landelin Amber Ale

TEMPURA BATTER

1/2	bottle St. Landelin Amber Ale
2	teaspoons dry yeast
2	teaspoons sugar
1–1 1/4	cup flour
2	tablespoons Japanese bread crumbs, available in specialty shops
1	tablespoon cornstarch (for bananas and cherries)

FRUIT

1	cup of fresh banana slices
1	cup of pitted fresh cherries

GARNISH

Fresh strawberries

Fresh basil (leaves)

Thin sugar cookies (as needed)

To prepare the sorbet, bring to a boil sugar, water, and wine in a sauce pot. Let boil for 10 minutes. remove from heat, add basil. Let cool and refrigerate over night. Next day, strain basil from sorbet base. Add the bottle of Amber Ale. Place in an ice-cream machine until frozen. Freeze at least two hours before you serve.

In a bowl, place the beer, yeast, and sugar. Let stand for 10 minutes. With a wire whisk, whip flour into beer until it is half the thickness for pancake batter. Let stand one hour in refrigerator. When ready to use, mix in Japanese bread crumbs. Sprinkle cornstarch over bananas and cherries, dip into batter and fry in 350°F oil until golden brown. For serving, place fried bananas and cherries in a bowl with a scoop of sorbet. Garnish with strawberry, fresh basil, and thin sugar cookies.

SERVES 6

"Beeramisu"

BILL KUNZ, GROWLER'S PUB, ST. LOUIS, MO

4   eggs, separated
4   tablespoons cane sugar
½   pound cream cheese
½   pound mascarpone cheese
¼   cup Grand Marnier
¾   cup (½ bottle) Flag Porter
1   package ladyfinger cookies
    shaved chocolate

Separate egg whites and yolks into 2 bowls. Place the egg whites in a metal bowl and beat until frothy. Then slowly add 2 tablespoons of the sugar as you continue to beat the egg whites until they form stiff peaks. Whip the yolks, then slowly add 2 tablespoons sugar and continue stirring until the sugar is dissolved and the yolks are a sunny yellow color. Add the Grand Marnier and 2 ounces of the Flag Porter and mix well. Add the cheeses to the yolk mixture and blend until smooth. Carefully fold the whipped egg whites into the yolk/cheese mixture.

Moisten the ladyfingers with the rest of the Flag Porter; do not allow them to become soggy. Place 3 moistened ladyfingers in the bottom of a bowl, top with ⅓ cup of cheese mixture, and spread evenly over the ladyfingers. Repeat for a second layer. Wrap and store until time to serve.

Present portions of the dessert on a small dessert plate topped with chocolate shavings.

SERVES 6

Fresh Cherry Bread Pudding

EXECUTIVE CHEF ANGELO J. GIORDANO,
THE OLD BAY RESTAURANT, NEW BRUNSWICK, NJ

2   cups pitted fresh cherries

3/4 cup Belgian red ale (Rhodenbach)

Half a loaf of sliced egg or challa bread (left out overnight to harden)

1/4 gallon whole milk

4   whole eggs

3/4 pound cane sugar

1/2 pound dark brown sugar

1/4 pound butter (softened)

2   tablespoons vanilla extract

1/2 cup chopped pecans

1/4 teaspoon cinnamon

1/4 teaspoon nutmeg

1/4 teaspoon allspice

Soak cherries in ale overnight, tossing occasionally. To prepare the sauce, place half the marinated cherries in a saucepan. Bring to a low simmer over medium low heat. Cook for 3 minutes. Remove from the heat and purée in a mixer or food processor until smooth. Chill slightly before serving on the bread pudding.

In a large bowl crumble the bread into small pieces (about 1-inch cubes). In another bowl whisk together the milk, eggs, sugar, butter, vanilla, pecans, spices, and half the marinated cherries, reserving the rest of the cherries for the sauce.

Coat a pan with nonstick oil spray. Preheat the oven to 350°F. Pour mixture over the bread and work together with your hands until all moisture is absorbed. Pour into prepared pan. Flatten mixture slightly and cover with foil. Place the covered pan in the oven and bake for 1½ hours. Remove the foil and cook until a knife inserted into the pudding comes out clean. Remove from oven and let cool for 1 hour. (This pudding reheats very well in a microwave oven.)

Serve warm with cherry sauce and a glass of Belgian red ale.

SERVES 6

Irish Stout Cake

CLARK NICKERSON, GRANITE BREWERY, TORONTO, ONTARIO, CANADA

2½ cups flour

1 cup sugar

3½ teaspoons baking soda

1½ teaspoons salt

2 eggs

1½ cups vegetable oil

½ cup fresh squeezed orange juice

¾ cups Irish stout

½ cup sultana raisins

½ cup currants

1 teaspoon ground ginger

1½ teaspoons cinnamon

1 teaspoon orange zest

Preheat oven to 400°F. Grease and flour a 10-inch springform pan (cheesecake pan). In a large mixing bowl, sift together flour, sugar, baking soda, and salt. In a separate bowl, mix eggs and oil. Alternating in thirds, add egg/oil mixture, orange juice, and stout to dry ingredients. Add remaining ingredients and mix well. Spoon in batter. Bake for approximately 50 minutes or until a knife, inserted into the middle of the cake, comes out clean. Cool for 3 hours. Top with toasted, sliced almonds.

MAKES 1 CAKE

Brooklyn Chocolate Imperial Stout Mousse

EXECUTIVE CHEF ANGELO J. GIORDANO,
THE OLD BAY RESTAURANT, NEW BRUNSWICK, NJ

1¼ pounds fine semi-sweet cooking chocolate, cut into small cubes

3 teaspoons powdered gelatin

4 ounces Brooklyn Chocolate Imperial Stout, chilled

1 quart heavy cream

7 eggs

3½ ounces cane sugar

2 ounces hot coffee
  Chocolate shavings

Place chocolate in a double boiler and melt, stirring occasionally. Set chocolate aside at room temperature. Next, "bloom" the gelatin (dissolve it) by stirring into the chilled beer and reserve at room temperature.

Whip heavy cream in an electric mixer until it forms soft peaks, remove from mixer, and refrigerate. Separate egg whites and yolks. In a mixer whip egg whites until frothy. As you continue mixing, slowly add sugar. Reserve in refrigerator.

Prepare gelatin by adding hot coffee to the gelatin/beer mixture. In a large bowl, add chocolate, gelatin mixture, and egg yolks. Mix until well blended. Fold this mixture into whipped cream. Fold egg whites into this mixture until smooth and consistent color (but still an airy, light mixture), do not overfold to the point that the mixture falls to a paste. Let set 2–4 hours in the refrigerator. Spoon into small bowls and serve topped with chocolate shavings–and a glass of Brooklyn Imperial Stout.

SERVES 12

Bourbon Stout Pecan Delight

JOE KUBIK,
JOHN HARVARD'S BREW HOUSE, CAMBRIDGE, MA

1¼ cup flour
½ teaspoon baking powder
½ teaspoon salt
1¼ cup pecans (finely chopped in a food processor)
⅓ cup sugar
1 stick (½ cup) butter

TOPPING
½ stick (¼ cup) melted butter
3 whole eggs, lightly beaten
1½ cup brown sugar (sifted)
3 tablespoon bourbon
1 teaspoon vanilla
¼ cup stout

Preheat oven to 350°F.

Sift the flour, baking powder, and salt. Add 1 cup of pecans (save ¼ cup for the topping). Cut the butter into cubes and cut into the mixture. (Cutting is a word used to describe the combining of a fat and a flour. The object is to arrive at a "rough meal" mixture. The butter should not be allowed to soften too much. There is a kitchen tool called a pastry cutter that is very easy to use.)

To prepare the topping mixture, melt the butter in a saucepan and add the eggs, sugar, bourbon, vanilla, and stout. Set aside. Evenly pat the flour mixture into a 9-inch well-greased square pan and bake until golden brown and puffed up. Remove from the oven and pour topping mixture on top, sprinkle with last ¼ cup of pecans and bake for about 25 minutes, or until liquid is set. Remove from oven and let cool. Run a knife around edges and unmold. Turn right side up, let cool, and cut into bar-shaped servings. Serve warm with or without ice cream or whipped cream.

MAKES 8–10 PIECES

Magic City Stout Shake

DON ALAN HANKINS,
THE MAGIC CITY BREWERY, BIRMINGHAM, AL

1   pint stout

2   scoops vanilla ice cream

1   teaspoon balsamic vinegar

Puree all ingredients in a blender. Serve in a tall glass.

SERVES 1

The Restaurant List

RESTAURANTS

ALDEN COUNTRY INN
1 Dorchester Road on The Common
Lyme, NH 03768
603.795.2222

ALLEN'S
143 Danforth St.
Toronto, Ontario M4K 1N2
CANADA
416.463.3086

**BIG RIVER GRILLE & BREWING
WORKS**
222 Broad Street
Chattanooga, TN 37402
615.267.2739

BISTROT BELGIQUE GOURMANDE
PO Box 5
302 Poplar Alley
Occoquan, VA 22125
703.494.1180
belgique@mnsinc.com
http://www.mnsinc.com/belgique

**BOSCOS PIZZA KITCHEN &
BREWERY**
7615 West Farmington Blvd.
Germantown, TN
901.756.7310

BRICKTOWN BREWERY
1 North Oklahoma Avenue
Oklahoma City, OK 73104
405.232.2739

BRISTOL BAR & GRILL
5400 West 119th St.
Leawood, KS 66209
913.663.5777

CITY TAVERN
3200 Filmore
San Francisco, CA 94123
415.567.0918

CUVE NOTREDAME
1701 Green
Philadelphia, PA 19130
215.765.2777

DENISON'S BREWING COMPANY
75 Victoria Street
Toronto, Ontario
CANADA
416.360.5877

**DOCK STREET BREWERY &
RESTAURANT**
1299 Pensylvania Avenue N.W.
Washington, DC 20004
202.639.0403

EDWARD MORANS BAR & GRILL
4 World Financial Center
New York, NY 10280
212.945.2255

EMPIRE BREWING
120 Walton St.
Syracuse, NY 13202
315.475.4400

FARMHOUSE RESTAURANT
1449 Chestnut Street
Emmaus, PA 18049
610.967.6225

FEARRINGTON HOUSE
2000 Fearrington Village Center
Pittsboro, NC 27312
919.542.2121

FRANK'S RESTAURANT
85 Tenth Avenue
New York, NY
212.243.1349

GRANITE BREWERY
245 Eglinton Avenue East
Toronto, Ontario M4P 3B7
CANADA
416.322.0723

GRITTY McDUFF'S
396 Fore Street
Portland, ME 04104
207.772.2739

GROWLER'S PUB
763 Old Ballas
St. Louis, MO 63141
314.429.5656

HARBOR BAY GOURMET
3714 South Ocean Boulevard
Stuart, FL 34996
407.286.9463

HEARTLAND BREWERY
35 Union Square West
New York, NY
212.645.3400

HOME RESTAURANT
20 Cornelia Street
New York, NY 10014
212.243.9579

THE INN AT MAPLEWOOD FARM
447 Center Road / P.O. Box 1478
Hillsborough, NH 03244
603.464.4242

JOHN HARVARD'S
33 Dunster St.
Cambridge, MA 02138
617.868.3585

KEENS CHOPHOUSE
72 West 36th Street
New York, NY 10018
212.947.3636

LANTANA GRILLE
The Pointe Hilton Resort on South
Mountain
Phoenix, AZ
602.431.6472

Le CHEVAL BLANC
809 Ontario East
Montreal, P.Q. H2J 3K3
CANADA
514.522.0211

THE MAGIC CITY BREWERY
420 21st South Street
Birmingham, AL 35233
205.328.2739

MIRACLE GRILL
112 First Avenue
New York, NY 10009
212.529.0215

NORTH PLANK ROAD TAVERN
18 North Plank Road
Newburgh, NY 12550
914.565.6885

OCEANA
55 East 54th Street
New York, NY 10022
212.759.5941

ODEON
145 West Broadway
New York, NY 10013
212.233.0507

OLD BAY RESTAURANT
61-63 Church Street
New Brunswick, NJ 08901
908.246.3111

OZARK BREWING COMPANY
43 West Dickson St.
Fayetteville, AR 72701
501.521.2739

PACIFIC NORTHWEST
322 Occidental Avenue South
Seattle, WA 98104
206.621.7002

PARKER HOUSE INN
16 Main Street
Quechee, VT 05059
802.295.6077

RIVER PLACE HOTEL
1510 Southwest Harbor Highway
Portland, OR 97201
503.228.3233

RITZ CARLTON ON AMELIA ISLAND
4750 Amelia Island Parkway
Amelia Island, Fl 32034
904.277.1100

R. P. McMURPHY'S
400 East Evergreen Blvd.
Vancouver, WA 98660
360.695.9211

SILO MICROBREWERY
630 Barret Ave.
Louisville, KY 40204
502.589.2739

SOUTHAMPTON PUBLICK HOUSE
40 Bowden Sq.
Southampton, NY 11946
516.283.2800

THE STANHOPE
995 Fifth Avenue
New York, NY 10028
212.288.5800

SWANS BREWPUB/ BUCKERFIELD'S BREWERY
506 Pandora Ave.
Victoria, B.C. V8W 1N6
604.361.3310

TIED HOUSE CAFE AND BREWERY
954 Villa Street
Mountain View, CA 94042
415.965.2739

TRIUMPH BREWING CO.
138 Nassau St.
Princeton, NJ 08542
609.924.7855

VIRGIL'S REAL BBQ
152 West 44th Street
New York, NY 10036
212.921.9494

WATERFRONT ALE HOUSE
136 Atlantic Avenue
Brooklyn, NY 11201
718.522.3794

WEBERS
845 South Montford Avenue
Baltimore, MD 21224
410.276.0800

WYNKOOP BREWING
1634 18th Street
Denver, CO 80202
303.297.2700

BREWERIES

The following breweries either offered assistance in my research, or are mentioned in the text by a chef. In the latter case, the statement cites either the brewery, or its products, as being of professional interest to the chef. (Brewery-restaurants are included in the restaurant list.)

James Koch
BOSTON BEER COMPANY
30 Germania Street
Boston, MA 02130
617.522.3400

Mary Harrison
BOULEVARD BREWING CO.
2501 Southwest Boulevard
Kansas City, MO 64108
816.474.7095

Bill May
BRICK BREWING CO. LTD.
181 King Street South
Waterloo, Ontario N2J 1P7
CANADA
519.576.0470

Jeff Close
CATAMOUNT BREWING CO.
58 South Main, P.O.Box 457
White River Junction, VT 05001
802.296.2248
802.296.2420

Loren Hart
HART BREWING CO. LTD.
#1 Brewery Lane
175 Industrial Avenue
Carlton Place, Ontario K7C 3V7
CANADA
613.253.4278

Peter Humes
HUMES BREWING CO.
2775 Cavedale Road
Glen Ellen, CA 95442
707.935.0723

Jack Joyce
ROGUE BREWERY
748 S.W. Bay Boulevard
Newport, OR 97365
503.265.2537

Denise Sposato
SHIPYARD BREWING CO.
86 Newbury Street
Portland, ME 04101
207.761.0807

APPENDIX 1
Weights and Measures

I. LARGER MEASURES OF CAPACITY

BARREL: For beer, usually 36 gallons, for wine 31.5 gallons

FIRKIN: For wine 84 gallons, for ale or beer 1/4 barrel or 9 gallons. (This is no mistake, the two firkins are indeed vastly different in size.)

GALLON: For ale 282 cu. in.; for wine 231 cu. in. Note that the 231 cu. in. wine gallon is identical to the U.S. gallon. This was the legal size of the gallon as established under Queen Anne in 1707. Also, the 282 cu. in. ale gallon is 1.65% larger than the 277.42 cu. in. Imperial gallon!

KILDERKIN: 18 gallons

PIN: 4.5 gallons

QUART:
Ale Quart: 70.50 cu. in.
Imperial Quart: 69.36 cu. in.
Reputed Quart: 46.24 cu. in. (i.e., 2/3 of the Imperial quart)
(Also known as the Whiskey quart)
Wine Quart: 57.75 cu. in. (i.e., the same as the U.S. quart)

QUARTER: 64 gallons, 1/4 of a tun

TUN: A measure of capacity for wine and ale, originally 256 gallons. For wine, the tun lost 4 gallons, and dropped to 252 gallons.

POTTLE: This term was used for 1/2 gallon in reference to beer.

II. DRINKING VESSELS AND BOTTLES

THURDENDEL: A drinking vessel, used in the seventeenth century, for malt liquors, somewhat larger that the requisite capacity so that a full measure of liquid may be obtained with the froth on top, similar in intent to the modern "line" beer glass.

"POUNDER": A colloquial expression used in reference to a 16 fl. ounce can of beer.

YARD: A drinking vessel measuring 36 inches from its base to its lip, featuring a large round base and a long tapered neck that flares quite wide at the top. This glass was originally used to provide coachmen their ale at stops, allowing the server to pass the vessel to the coachman without the coachman having to get down off the coach. The capacity varies, but 2.5 pints and 4.5 pints are the most common sizes.

Today, the yard is a novelty that can be found in a number of fine pubs. In many cases, the yard is used in drinking contests, particulary those involving timed consumption. The *Guinness Book of Records* last reported records for such a contest in 1990. Half-yard and foot glasses of the same style exist.

LINE GLASS: A glass with the rated capacity shown as a line near the top of the glass.

III. SMALL MEASURES: U.S., U.K., AND METRIC EQUIVALENTS

Name	Sys Abbrev.	Ounces	cc/ml
gallon	U.S. gal	128	3785.413
quart	U.S. qt	32	946.353
pint	U.S. pt	16	473.177
gill	U.S. gi	4	118.294
fluid ounce	U.S. fl oz	1	29.574
fluid dram	U.S. fl dr	1/8	3.69669
gallon	U.K. gal	160	4546
quart	U.K. qt	40	1136
pint	U.K. pt	20	568.26
gill	U.K. gi	5	142.066
fluid ounce	U.K. fl oz	1	28.412
fluid dram	U.K. fl dr	1/8	3.5516

APPENDIX 2
Alcohol Content

When Prohibition was repealed, the power to regulate alcohol was granted to the individual states. Thus, it varies greatly from one state to another. The only exception to this rule is the federal regulation on container labeling. In the United States you can label any fermented malt beverage as "beer" as long as it is less than 5% alcohol by volume. Anything over 5% alcohol by volume must be labeled as "malt liquor." Regular beer and malt liquor are not brewing terms, but as far as the federal government is concerned, if you brew a lager that is 5%, it is a beer, if it is 5.1%, it is a malt liquor.

A "typical" beer contains between 4.5% and 5% alcohol by volume (or about 3.5–4% alcohol by weight). The norm for the U.S. megabrewery products (~4% by weight) is the same as for Canadian megabrewery products (~5% by volume). For some reason, people don't seem to believe it, though. It's a frequent mistake made by those "documenting" that Canadian beers are stronger than American beers. Just for the record, it is possible to brew beers with alcohol contents ranging from negligible (less than 3% abv) to very potent [Sam Adams Triple Bock (sic) at around 17% abv]. As an example, consider how many people are convinced that Canadian or German or English or (insert country of choice here) beers are much more alcoholic than American beers.

Glossary

ADJUNCT: An ingredient used in the grist, or added to the wort, that is not malted barley. Examples of adjuncts are: corn, rice, sugar, wheat, and other cereal grains. Adjuncts are used to alter flavors or because of economic reasons. In some cases, such as Belgian Lambic beers, fruit is added to create unique beers such as kriek (cherries), framboise (raspberries), and peche (peach).

AEROBIC: The word used to describe an organism, such as a top-fermenting ale yeast, that needs oxygen to metabolize.

ALCOHOL (ETHENOL): (C$_2$H$_5$OH) The by-product of fermentation. The result of yeast metabolizing sugar.

ALCOHOL BY VOLUME: A measurement of the alcohol content of a solution in terms of the percentage volume of alcohol per volume of beer.

To approximately calculate the volumetric alcohol content, subtract the final gravity from original gravity and divide the result by 7.5 (margin of error +/- 15 %).

ALCOHOL BY WEIGHT: A measurement of the alcohol content of a solution in terms of the percentage weight of alcohol per volume of beer. Example: 3.2 percent alcohol by weight is equal to 3.2 grams of alcohol per 100 centiliters of beer.

The percent of alcohol by weight figure is approximately 20% lower than the "by volume" figure because alcohol weighs less than its equivalent volume of water.

ALE: A beverage made from malted barley, hops, and water, fermented with a top-fermenting (aerobic) yeast, at a relatively high temperature. Adjuncts can be added, as deemed necessary, to meet the color, flavor, and alcohol content requirements to be brewed in a specific "style." (See chapter on Beer Styles.)

ALTBIER: A style of beer from the Dusseldorf region of Germany that is fermented using a top fermenting (ale) yeast and cold conditioned. (Contrast Steam Beer: lager yeast fermented and conditioned at ale temperatures.)

ANAEROBIC: A word used to describe an organism, such as a bottom-fermenting lager yeast, that is able to metabolize in the absence of oxygen.

ATTENUATION: The degree to which the beer has fermented; the final gravity expressed as a percentage of the original specific gravity.

BARLEY: A cereal grain that is malted for use in the grist that becomes the mash in the process of brewing beers.

BARLEYWINE: A brew with a high original gravity (up to 11% alcohol by volume). Commercially available examples are Anchor Old Foghorn and Sierra Nevada Bigfoot.

BARREL: A standard of measurement equal to 31 U.S. gallons. In Britain, a standard of measurement equal to 36 Imperial gallons (43.2 U.S. gallons).

BEER: A fermented beverage made from grain, hops water, yeast, and, in some cases, additional adjuncts.

BIERE DE GARDE: A beer from the northern part of France. Originally made by farmers in the region, these beers are a little over 8% alcohol by volume. They have a medium hop flavoring with slight traces of spice (cinnamon, nutmeg), and a touch of apple or pear.

BITTER: A subclassification of traditional pale ale, with less hops and carbonation that a traditional pale ale. The distinction between bitter and pale ale has become less and less over the years. Today English brewers have difficulty telling where to draw the line.

BOCK: A dark, strong (6–7% alcohol content by volume) lager-style beer, first brewed in the city of Einbeck (pronounced Ein-bock) in Bavaria, Germany, in the fourteenth and fifteenth centuries. This style was brewed to survive shipment throughout Europe.

BODY: The consistency of the beer. It is described as full-bodied, medium-bodied, or light-bodied. The relative descriptions are used when tasting beers and are usually used in comparison with another beer.

BREW KETTLE: Also called *copper*, it is the vessel in which wort is boiled with the hops after mashing and before chilling and fermentation.

BREWPUB: A brewery/restaurant where the beer brewed on premise is dispensed directly from bright tanks for consumption on premise only.

BRIGHT TANK: The pressurized fermentation vessel where the beer is kept, chilled, and under pressure, until drawn off by the person operating the tap in the brewpub. In a traditional brewery it is used to store beer prior to bottling or kegging.

BROWN ALE: The most famous English brown ale is Newcastle Brown Ale. Other ales of the same type are brewed in the northern part of England. They are nutty in flavor with mild hopping.

CAMRA: An organization in England that was founded in the mid-1960s to preserve the production of cask-conditioned beers and ales.

CARAMEL: A cooked sugar that is used to add color and alcohol content to beer. It is often used in place of more expensive malted barley.

CARBON DIOXIDE: The gas by-product of yeast metabolism during fermentation when simple sugars are broken down into alcohol and gas. Under pressure, carbon dioxide causes effervescence in beer.

CASK: Container for draft beer that is designed for beer dispensed at atmospheric pressure. "Cask-conditioned" beers are allowed to finish conditioning in the cask and are served by gravity tap, not under pressure.

CREAM ALE: A beer specific to North America, usually a lager fermented product with a relatively high alcohol and hop content.

CONDITIONING: The process that causes beer to become effervesent.

COPPER: The large (usually copper) vessel where the wort is boiled with the hops before being chilled and piped into the fermentation tanks. Copper was used because it heats evenly and does not chemically react to the beer while it is boiled with the hops.

DORTMUNDER: Named after the city in Germany where this beer is brewed, this is a malty, rich, lightly hopped lager beer with a golden color. It is lighter and less aromatic than a pilsner.

DEXTRIN: The unfermentable substance made by the enzymes found naturally in barley, these substances give beer its flavor, body, and mouth-feel. By controlling the temperature during the mash, the brewmaster can determine how much dextrin is produced. Lower temperatures tend to develop more dextrin, while higher temperatures convert the starches to more sugar than dextrin. It gives the beer its "mouth-feel". Without it, beer would taste thin

DRAFT (DRAUGHT): The process of dispensing beer from a bright tank, cask, or keg, by hand-pump, by pressure from an air pump, or by injected carbon dioxide.

DUNKEL. From the German word meaning "dark." This term is used especially in terms of Weiss beers. There are many very famous "Dunkel" wheat beers brewed in the German city of Munich.

ENZYMES: Catalysts that are found naturally in the grain of the barley cereal. When heated in a mash, it converts the starches of the malted barley into maltose, a sugar used in solution, and fermented, to make beer.

ESTERS: Aromatic oils that are the by-products of fermentation. These are especially prevalent in the metabolization of sugars by top-fermenting ale yeasts. Their characteristic "fruity" aromas are the sign of a well fermented ale. (Aromatics include apple, pear, pineapple, prune, and the aroma of new-mown hay or lawn grass.)

FARO: Faro is a young lambic that is sweetened and sometimes spiced; when bottled, it's usually pasteurized to keep the added sugar from fermenting.

FRAMBOISE: A Belgian lambic in which ripe raspberries have been added to the fermentation. The raspberries add a refreshing flavor to the rather dry and slightly sour beer.

GRAVITY (SPECIFIC GRAVITY): The amount of materials (usually sugars) in ratio to a specific measure of water expressed as a percentage. If a specific solution of water and maltose consists of equal parts of sugar and water, the specific gravity is said to be 1.050 or, in brewer's terms, 50 SG. More traditionally, commercial brewers use the terms Balling, or Plato, and measure the weight of sugar in solution as a percentage of the weight of the solution (grams per 100 grams of solution).

GRIST: The crushed grains used to make a mash. The grist can consist of any number of grains (barely malt, corn, rice, oatmeal…) except in Bavaria, where the Rheinheitsgebot, or Purity Law, decrees that only malted barley can be used.

GUEUZE: A blend of young and old lambic beers are bottled and allowed to continue fermentation in the bottle. The result is a very effervescent dry beer, not unlike champagne.

HEFE-: A German word meaning "with." Used mostly in conjunction with wheat (Weiss) beers to denote that the beer is bottled or kegged with the yeast in suspension (Hefe-weiss). These beers are cloudy, frothy, and very refreshing.

HOP: The flowering herb used to flavor and preserve beer. First used in Flanders in the fifteenth century, its use spread rapidly, mainly for its preservative effect on beers that were being shipped long distances.

INDIA PALE ALE: The name given to a high gravity (7–8% alcohol by volume) pale ale that was intentionally well hopped so that it could survive the long voyage from the United Kingdom to the far-reaching military and economic outposts of that Empire.

KEG: One-half barrel, or 15.5 U.S. gallons.

KRAEUSEN: The addition of fermenting wort to a fermented beer during lagering. The result is a burst of fermentation and an increase in effervescence.

KRIEK: A Belgian lambic beer that has been fermented with ripe cherries in the primary fermentation. The fruit adds a balance to the slightly sour flavor of the lambic.

LAGER: A German word meaning "to store." Used in reference to the storage of bottom fermented beers.

LAMBIC: A beer from the area in, and around, Bruxelles, Belgium. The fermentation of this malted barley and malted wheat beer is the result of actions of ambient yeast.

LENGTH: The amount of wort brewed each time the brewhouse is in operation.

LIQUOR: The brewers' word for water used in the brewing process as included in the mash, or used to sparge the grains after mashing. A traditional phrase used by brewers to differentiate between water and liquor is: "Liquor goes in the beer, water washes the beer off the floor."

MAIBOCK: Traditionally brewed in the

spring, this is a strong beer brewed to last in "lager" until the fall. This beer is a traditional beer of Bavaria and is associated with Oktoberfest.

MALT(ING): A process that develops the starch content of grain.

MALT EXTRACT: The condensed wort from a mash, consisting of maltose, dextrins, and other dissolved solids. Either as a syrup or powdered sugar, it is used by brewers, in solutions of water and extract, to reconstitute wort for fermentation.

MALT LIQUOR: A term used in the United States to designate a fermented malt beverage of relatively high alcohol content (7-8% by volume).

MALTOSE: The sugar derived from mashing barley malt. This sugar is metabolized by yeast to produce beer.

MARZEN: Very close to a Vienna-style beer, these beers are brewed especially for the Oktoberfest held in late September/early October in Munich. These beers are "session" beers that are amber in color and semi-dry.

MASH: The combination of grist and liquor, heated to a specific temperature for the optimum production of maltose and other nonfermentable products (dextrins).

MICROBREWERY: A brewery that produces less than 15,000 barrels of beer a year.

MOUTH-FEEL: The experience of feeling the body of the beer while tasting it. (Also see Body.)

OKTOBERFEST: In 1810, the first Oktoberfest was held in the city's "village green" to celebrate the wedding of Prince Luitpold of Bavaria and his bride the Bavarian Queen Theresia. It was such a fun wedding that the citizens of Munich have celebrated it every year since (with only two or three years when political and military events overshadowed the celebration). Today the green is known as the Theresienwiese (Wies'n) and the "March Beer" (brewed in March and tapped for the Oktoberfest) is since then called "Wies'n Beer."

PALE ALE: A traditional beer brewed in the United Kingdom. This is an amber colored, very lightly hopped top-fermented brew. The most famous pale ale was, and still is, Bass.

PASTEURIZATION: Heating a liquid to kill spoilage microorganisms, to render it sterile. The process is used on beer to increase the shelf-life of the product and stop all fermentation that might still be going on in the solution.

PILZEN: The name of a city in the Czech Republic that first began brewing this clear, golden, bottom-fermented beer. The most famous example of this style of beer is Pilsner Urquel.

PITCHING: A word used to describe the action of adding yeast to a chilled wort in preparation for fermentation.

PORTER: Similar to a Stout, but a lighter, less intense beer, with a very deep garnet color and a smooth, less astringent flavor than stout. Once a "dead" beer, this style of beer has been reborn thanks to the microbreweries in the United States.

RAUCHBIER: A German word (rauch/smoke and bier/beer) used to describe beer that is made from malted barley that has been smoked in a way similar to the process used in Scotland to produce smoked grain for the production of Scotch whiskey. A famous rauchbier is produced in the city of Wurtzburg in Franconia, an area in central Germany.

SCOTCH ALE: A strong (6–10% alcohol by volume), sweet, full-bodied ale brewed in Scotland. Although this is called an "ale" it is brewed much closer to a lager-style beer: fermented at low temperatures and lagered for up to 6 months.

SPECIFIC GRAVITY: (See GRAVITY)

STEAM BEER: A beer indigenous to San Francisco in the nineteenth and early twentieth centuries. It is an amber beer fermented with bottom-fermenting (lager) yeast at relatively high temperatures. Legend has it that the name came from the process of rebunging kegs of the beer. During the process the fermenting beer would erupt from the bung hole and was called "steam" by the brewers.

STOUT: A name acquired by very dark porter beers. The name was adopted by the Guinness brewing company in Ireland for a dark beer it called "Stout Porter." In time, the "porter" part of the name was dropped in favor of "Stout."

TRAPPIST ALES: These are top-fermented, bottled-conditioned, usually slightly sweet ales brewed by Trappist monks. There are only six true Trappist breweries (five in Belgium and one in the Netherlands): Chimay, Orval, Rochefort, Westmalle, and Sint Sixtus at Westvleteren in Belgium, and Schaapskooi at Koningshoeven in the Netherlands. Only a beer made at a Trappist monastery can officially use the word "Trappist" in the name of its beer.

VIENNA BEER: In the nineteenth century, this amber lager beer was the toast of Vienna, Austria. Today, there is only one major brewery producing a Vienna-style beer, and that brewery is in Mexico. The beer is called Dos Equis.

WEISSE: A German word meaning "white" or "wheat," depending on the context. Weissebier is a particular favorite of the Bavarian brewers of Munich. All six of the major breweries in that city brew at least two weisse-beers.

WORT: The sweet liquid made up of maltose, liquor, and hop flavoring which is fermented to make beer.

YEAST: A single-celled fungi of the genus *Saccharomyces*.

Beer Index

Chef Index

Recipe Index

Restaurant Index (by Name)

Restaurant Index (by State)

NEW YORK (State) *(continued)*
    North Plank Road Tavern, Newburgh,
        44, 159, 160, 161, 167, 182
    Southhampton Publick House,
        Southampton, 33, 144, 183
    Waterfont Ale House, Brooklyn, 84,
        130, 183
NORTH CAROLINA
    Fearrington House, Pittsboro, 37, 126,
        182
OKLAHOMA
    Bricktown Brewery, Oklahoma City,
        85, 101, 128, 153, 181
OREGON
    River Place Hotel, Portland, 97, 147, 183
PENNSYLVANIA
    Cuve Notredame, Philadelphia, 41,
        107, 181

TENNESSEE
    Boscos, Germantown, 78, 96, 122,
        149, 171, 181
    Big River Grille & Brewing Works,
        Chattanooga, 27, 28, 91, 105, 136,
        137, 172, 181
VERMONT
    Parker House Inn, Quechee, 40, 50,
        54, 68, 74, 120, 183
VIRGINIA
    Bistrot Belgique Gourmande,
        Occoquan, 93, 141, 181
WASHINGTON
    R.P. McMurphy's, 92, 183

General Index

Raisonettes™, 32
Rauch (smoked beer), 43
Rauchbier (style), 22, 194
Red Beans and Rice with Andouille
    Sausage, 79, 154
Red Dog, 44
Redhook Ale, 91
Rice, 44
    Texmati, Herb Rice, 161
    Sushi Rice, 168
Rice maker, 89
Rice, Otto (chef), 92
Riptides (restaurant), 34
Ritz Carlton on Amelia Island, 31, 103,
    183
River Place Hotel, 97, 147, 183
Rodenbach Red, 60, 70
Rogue Dry Hopped Red, 62
    Rogue Mogul Madness, 66
    Rogue Nut Brown Nectar, 52
    Rogue Old Crustacean, 62, 64
Rolling Rock, 86
Roux, 115
R.P. McMurphy's (restaurant), 92, 183
Rupertsburg (Germany), 10
Russian Black Bread, 106, 170
Russo, Dan (chef), 86, 101, 134, 183

Sabakaido (The Mackeral Rout), 89
Saba sushi, 89
Saccharomyces cervisiae, 7
Saccharomyces uvarum, 7
Saison Dupont, 52
Salmon
    Baked with Hefe-Weizen, Sweet Corn,
        and Fennel, 86, 131
    (Norwegian) Fillet in Honey Porter,
        87, 132
    Tartare Wrapped with Smoked
        Salmon, 86, 133
Sauce
    Swans Arctic Ale Cream Sauce, 165

Vin-blanc, 132
Sam Adams Beer Dinner (menu), 58
Samichlaus Bier, 22, 66, 107
Samuel Adams Boston Lager, 58
Samuel Adams Cherry Wheat, 58, 103
Samuel Adams Golden Pilsner, 58
Samuel Adams Honey Porter, 58
Samuel Adams Summer Ale, 58
Samuel Adams Triple Bock, 58
Samuel Smith Pale Ale, 52
Sausages with Caramelized Onions and
    Apples, 100, 153
Schagrin, Jeff (chef), 104, 167
Schierlinger Roggen, 46, 60
Schlitz, Joseph, 13
Schmidt, Alan, 41
Schultheiss Berliner Weisse, 60
Scott & Jamie's Texas Lovers' Chili, 80,
    146
Scottish ale (style), 17, 194
Seattle (WA), 38
Sedivy, Jack (chef), 79, 121, 154
Sedlmeyer, Gabriel, 14
Shrimp
    Ale-Battered, and Onion Rings, 85, 135
    Fiery Shrimp, 86, 134
    Shrimp Shell Soup, 77, 126
Sierra Nevada Celebration Ale (1995),
    46, 52
Sierra Nevada Pale Ale, 64
Silo Microbrewery, 79, 121, 154, 183
Simoes, Laura (chef), 87, 123, 168, 169
Simpson, Wade (chef), 40, 79, 127, 142,
    173
Smoked beer (style), 22
Southampton (NY), 33, 144, 183
Southampton Publick House, 33, 144, 183
Southampton Village, 34, 144, 183
Sparging, 8
Spaten Premium Lager, 30, 46
Specialty beers (style), 21
Spicy Cheese and Lager Dip, 119

Yeast, 7, 194
Yeungling Porter, 19
Yorkville Brewery (NY), 34

Zenger, John (chef), 97, 147, 183